APPLIED
THEATRE

APPLIED THEATRE

Creating Transformative Encounters in the Community

Philip Taylor
New York University

HEINEMANN
Portsmouth, NH

Heinemann

361 Hanover Street
Portsmouth, NH 03801–3912
www.heinemanndrama.com

Offices and agents throughout the world

Library of Congress Cataloging-in-Publication Data
Taylor, Philip.
  Applied theatre : creating transformative encounters in the
  community / Philip Taylor.
    p. cm.
  Includes bibliographical references.
  ISBN 0-325-00535-4
1. Theater and society. 2. Community theater. I. Title.
PN2049.T38 2003
792—dc21   2003001549

Editor: Lisa A. Barnett
Production: Elizabeth Valway
Cover design: Jenny Jensen Greenleaf
Composition: Publishers' Design and Production Services, Inc.
Manufacturing: Steve Bernier

Printed in the United States of America on acid-free paper
Sheridan 2019

To Lowell, Nancy, and 76 Washington Place

CONTENTS

CONTENTS

FOREWORD

Certain latter-day philosophers have suggested with chagrin that the dominant project of Western philosophy has been a quest for the objective and permanent ideals of Truth, Goodness, and Beauty. This quest has been engaged in by a special class of thinkers and experts who presume themselves best equipped to guide the rest of us toward those enduring ideals. They have included aestheticians who have earnestly applied themselves to the task of discriminating between the truly beautiful and the not-so. Many have insisted that genuinely artistic products—formally wondrous, ethereal objects lounging in an aesthetic remove—possess an inherent beauty, one that is independent of and unmarred by the mundane happenings of everyday life. Only professional connoisseurs who focus away from the debilitating world of experience, with its ugly affairs of politics and commerce, can gain full access to the bedazzling interplay of formal qualities inherent within those works of art.

Some thinkers, of course have dissented from this tradition of thought. One who begged to differ with this idealist view of the world, and of the nature of art, was the great American pragmatist philosopher John Dewey. Dewey's fullest and most powerful articulation of his counterposition to classical aesthetics is found in his book *Art as Experience*. In this book, Dewey ([1934] 1958) eloquently challenged the traditional distancing of the aesthetic from the everyday; he asked:

> Why is there repulsion when the high achievements of fine art are brought into connection with common life, the life that we share with all living creatures? Why is life thought of as an affair of low appetite, or at its best a thing of gross sensation, and ready to sink from its best to the level of lust and harsh cruelty? (20)

Arguing for an end to the segregation of the aesthetic from the mundane, he asked his readers to see art as coterminous with being in the world, to see it as "prefigured within the very process of living" (Dewey [1934] 1958, 24).

John Dewey, in *Art as Experience* and elsewhere, rarely aimed his philosophical ruminations specifically at the art of the theatre.

Nevertheless, I cite Dewey here because his spirit (along with that of one other philosopher to be revealed shortly) seemed to hover over my reading of Philip Taylor's book about an intriguing and decidedly nontraditional approach to the theatrical arts.

Indeed, until relatively recently, the theatre has, in many ways, represented that of the Greeks. Theatre in the Western world has been bound by the formal constraints of literature, its texts scripted by members of a playwright class. It has insisted on a distance between actors and spectators, the action occurring on a stage, drawing attention to the difference in the reality of the onlooking audience and the imaginary world of the play. The audience is positioned as essentially passive recipients of a self-contained object of beauty that is *rounded out* from prologue to exodus, from entrance to denouement.

Historians of the theatre point to the European avant-garde movement, including the work of the dadaists, as posing an early challenge to the traditionally passive spectatorship of the audience. Later, especially in the late 1950s and the 1960s, experimental performances known as *events*, *happenings*, erupted within and around—rather than in front of—an arena audience. The 1970s and 1980s brought to the fore another set of theatrical aesthetics (in, for example, *body art*) that often disposed of story in favor of a fusion of the visual and the aural with the performing arts.

Then in the early 1990s, certain sociologists and anthropologists began to experiment with artistic presentations of their data. Some adaptations of ethnographies moved beyond dramatic scripts shaped out of data gathered in field texts and performed by researchers, to an involvement of the inhabitants of researched communities in the production of plays about local issues for other members of the community. Finally, Taylor himself mentions the learning-through-drama movement that shifted performances into *real-world* educational and therapeutic settings, thereby promoting the connections between art and the "affairs of common life" of which Dewey so eloquently wrote.

Applied theatre, too, moves to collapse the classical dichotomy of aesthetic form and content as it defies the distance between the admirable but essentially useless work of art and the substantial problems of life in the trenches. Those trenches—or, in Taylor's apt term, *aesthetic platforms*—can, he notes, be found in (among other places) prisons, community arts centers, and housing and industrial sites. These are places where real problems reside, where the materials of the artist are close at hand, and where genuine education can occur.

Indeed, the most obvious confluence of the thinking of John Dewey with the applied theatre work described and championed by Taylor appears in the latter's insistence that the theatre reside at the intersection of education and the arts. The arts are seen as a set of media with a potential for promoting profoundly educational experiences. They can allow for everyday concerns, so close and yet so distant, to be freshly apprehended and deeply felt, to be perceived (perhaps for the first time) as problems that must be addressed. Dewey ([1934] 1958) equated this sort of *seeing anew* with an "act of reconstructive doing" wherein consciousness becomes fresh and alive. And this reconstruction lives at the heart of every aesthetic and truly educational experience, enacted in places where good teachers are artists and good artists are teachers.

In this wise and useful book by Philip Taylor, Dewey's thoughts about the arts in general are indeed given a home in the more bounded territory of the theatre. But Taylor's hopes for a theatre, which can be critical, participatory, community-based, and ultimately socially and personally transformative, move beyond Dewey's less overtly political brand of aesthetics into one with a more explicit awareness of the power relationships that exist within all human projects. Taylor himself recognizes the work of Bertolt Brecht and Augusto Boal as prominent sources of influence on his thinking about desirable goals for the theatrical arts. These champions of a socially conscientious theatre do indeed provide broad shoulders for later theorists and practitioners such as Taylor to stand on as they further explore the possibilities of a theatre of, by, and for the people.

But if Taylor's notion of an applied theatre recalls Dewey's efforts at repairing the unfortunate dichotomy between the artistic and the commonplace, his vision of the arts as a means for intervening in the history of a community of people summons up the early writings of the great philosopher Jean-Paul Sartre. Sartre (1988) focused first on the novel as he imagined a socially engaged literature (*littérature engagée*), but later expanded his interests to include the writing and production of plays and screenplays. Arts of all sorts, suggested Sartre, must be aimed not merely toward "pure contemplative enjoyment," but seen as "the instruments of possible action." Indeed, Sartre (1988) wrote: "The world and man reveal themselves by their undertakings. And all the undertakings we speak of reduce themselves to a single one, making history" (55). Theatre that makes history, then, is one that embraces the possibility of enhancing social justice—or promoting, as Sartre would have it, greater freedom for all mankind.

One can hardly avoid a similar sentiment in reading *Applied Theatre*. Taylor's applied theatre is indeed devoted to the transformation of debilitating social conditions through reflection and action on the nature and sources of those conditions. But Taylor also imagines a theatre that is Sartrean in another sense. Like Sartre's engaged literature, Taylor's brand of applied theatre repudiates heavy-handed polemics. Neither finds acceptable the promulgation of the sort of final, correct interpretation of events that is the hallmark of propaganda.

Sartre (1988) put it this way: "in committed literature, commitment must in no way lead to a forgetting of literature." While, for Sartre, the literary text was fundamentally a rhetorical device, its aim was seen as gently enticing the reader to reconsider the political and historical realities of a particular situation. Similarly, Taylor writes of theatre that is a catalyst for reflection and inquiry, one that poses problems rather than closing down interpretive options, one that "seeks incompleteness [and] . . . demonstrates possible narratives." His notion of an applied theatre thus strikes an affirmative postmodernist note as it moves to challenge the control of the (however right-minded) playwright over the meanings to be extracted from his or her script. In this democratic approach to theatre, authorial/authoritative monologue is replaced by an intersubjective conversation in which interpretive power is shared. Or as Taylor writes (57):

> I am at my most confident when I see an applied theatre project in which participants are permitted to dialogue, to argue, to press a point, to interrogate the logic of any given action. Divergence should be welcomed in the applied theatre because the solutions teaching artists may be inclined to make might have no greater currency or accuracy than those of the participants.

This telling passage, among others, reveals Taylor's allegiance to a truly democratic theatre. Indeed, this book's author, like Sartre, consistently demonstrates a profound interest in intervening in history, but always through an art-making process that embodies the very democratic values that are themselves the ends of that intervention.

One final parallel between Sartre's engaged literature and the applied theatre described here lies in a mutual respect for particulars as important companions to theoretical abstractions. The power of literature, suggested Sartre, lies partly in its capacity to move beyond theory, and the mere designation of objective realities, toward the evocation of specific images that can be directly sensed and thereby reexperienced. The deep understandings evoked by works of art, especially narrative and performance art, are the result of their embodying precisely drawn virtual worlds into which otherwise mere onlookers are enticed, if only for a moment, to live vicariously. These virtual worlds create a safe distance from which that temporary inhabitant may be encouraged to revisit analogous, sometimes oppressive, conditions in their daily experiences, and to consider possible means of transforming those real-world contingencies.

In *Applied Theatre*, Taylor does more than advance a theory about theater—although, as I have suggested, that is well attended to. Equally important, Taylor provides numerous vividly etched examples that illustrate what he is proposing. The inclusion of these examples adds enormous weight to this book because they ground the author's theoretical arguments for community-based theater in actual theatrical productions. For me, the general and the particular here achieves a kind of synergy, emerging as a powerful dialectic that served to advance my understanding of what theater can be and can do.

Indeed, in this remarkable and timely book, Philip Taylor moves to rescue the theatrical arts from those debilitating features that characterize less-than-truly-democratic versions of this important art form. Taylor does not insist that his notion of applied theater exclude other possibilities in and for the field. But this book left me hopeful that the theater can at least occasionally extricate itself from conventions that have permeated Western culture for too long. I am convinced that *Applied Theatre*—like applied theatre, itself—can perform a similar service for other readers and theater lovers, unleashing us from our constrained vision of what the arts, in general, and the theatre, in particular, can be and of what they can help us become.

—Tom Barone

REFERENCES

Dewey, J. [1934] 1958. *Art as Experience.* New York: Capricorn Books.

Sartre, J. P. 1988. *What Is Literature? And Other Essays.* Cambridge: Harvard University Press.

ACKNOWLEDGMENTS

I would like to acknowledge my colleagues at New York University for supporting me in writing this text. I would especially note the support I have received from Dr. Lawrence Ferrara, Chair, Department of Music and Performing Arts Professions, The Steinhardt School of Education, New York University. I have had the opportunity of working with many outstanding teaching artists whose work continues to inspire me. I am grateful to all of the students I have taught whose insights have sharpened my analysis. The field of applied theatre is an evolving one and, although many of the ideas contained here are in a state of evolution, I would not have been able to get this far without the dedication of those who have preceded me. I especially acknowledge all those artist educators who have been tireless in their enthusiasm to take theatre out of the mainstream houses into various field settings so that the quality of all of our lives can be transformed into something better, whatever that *better* may be.

ACKNOWLEDGMENTS

INTRODUCTION:
THE APPLIED THEATRE

In a densely populated urban center, a terrorist attack of unprecedented proportions occurs. Two thousand people lose their lives
as hijacked aircraft explode into dual towering office buildings;
flaming buildings can be seen from across the city and beyond. A
panic grips the city as details slowly emerge. Schools and offices
are closed, hospitals are on standby, transit services are canceled,
telephone services are out of order. Could this really be happening?

News of those who work in or near the site of the attack is desperately sought by relatives and friends. The media relays the pain
and suffering to the world and stories slowly emerge of those
trapped in the office buildings. News of the horrible choices: to
jump from the 100th floor of a towering inferno or to die from asphyxiation? The sight of people falling to their deaths, the thud of
their bodies landing on the terrace roofs, haunts the soul.

As the weeks go by, the city's survivors tell about what they remember of that day, of the planes flying overhead, dangerously low,
of being caught on a bus with nowhere to go, of desperately trying
to give blood and food, of forcing one's way to the destruction site
to volunteer to help, of the caustic dust, of the seeming end of
the world. Information gathers—the terrorists were trained in the
country they attacked, they assimilated in the community, and
they played a game of make-believe and conned all those around
them that they were good community members, not community
destroyers.

Life has changed, little seems certain. Some cultural groups are
isolated by vigilantes, counterattacks are entertained, and retribution begins.

Within this context, eight million residents try and pick up the
pieces of their lives. Parents search for the words to answer their
children's questions; lost loved ones have not been recovered
from the attack site—now referred to as Ground Zero. Some families whose husbands, wives, sons, and daughters were murdered
do not have human remains to bury, some are lucky if a finger is

recovered, perhaps a skull fragment. DNA testing helps identify a few, so few, recoveries.

When schools reopen, there is the painful duty of processing this horrible incident with children who witnessed the events firsthand, many of whom are traumatized by the terrorism, as are their teachers. In other cities' workplaces, employee absenteeism is high. For those who go back to work, concentration is low, motivation is lagging, but the need to take one's mind off the incident is essential. The city supports programs to help residents talk openly about that day, encouraging them to air their fears and their grief. As they process their loss, the arts become even more important experiences for the community.

Applied theatre work, in which artists generate scenarios and create opportunities for the community to respond to their pain, is commissioned. In a local elementary school, children tell stories of how it was for them to witness the events firsthand from their classroom window. They render their stories into dramatic form. Play texts, which serve as catalysts for discussion and for further theatre work, are written. Audiences who observe this work share their own stories in postperformance workshops.

Theatre becomes a way for community members to examine their relationship to the shocking events of the attack. In this new version of community theatre, people can directly apply the art form to assist in reconstructing their identities. Community theatre is vital to the process of healing for it enables people to share pain and hope narratives.

The community theatre is an applied theatre form in which individuals connect with and support one another and where opportunities are provided for groups to voice who they are and what they aspire to become. Applied theatre becomes a medium through which storytellers can step into the perspectives of others and gain entry points to different worldviews—perspectives that might even articulate why the events of that day of barbarity might have occurred. This theatre shares much in common with other theatre movements in which the art form is central to storytelling, to healing, to teaching, and to learning. Participatory theatre, interactive theatre, theatre in education, theatre of the oppressed, community theatre, outreach theatre, theatre for development—all are interested in the applications of a reflective theatre, a theatre that is concerned with facilitating dialogue on who we are and what we aspire to become. In the words of Michael Rodd (1988):

> The theatre allows us to converse with our souls—to passionately pursue and discover ways of living with ourselves and others. We are all artists, and theatre is a language. We have no better way to work together, to learn about each other, to heal and to grow. (xix)

APPLIED THEATRE TEACHES US TO TEACH OTHERS

On the other side of the world, in a rural township two hundred miles from the closest urban center, another community is suffering a crisis—a different version of Ground Zero. Unemployment is depressingly high with many adults disenchanted by their desperate and frustrating search for work, work that doesn't exist. Alarming increases in the use of antidepressant medication, especially among young males, is occurring. Domestic violence has reached staggering proportions and incidences of physical and verbal harassment are at an all-time high. Single-parent families are common and notions of a regular household income are laughable. Families live from day to day, week to week, dependent on assistance from social security and other outreach services. Drug and alcohol abuse is a virtual industry among young people.

In this particular community, suicide, especially teenage suicide, is seen as a positive solution to life's problems. Government departments have directed their officers in health, housing, and education programs to prioritize community initiatives to try to directly combat how suicide could be seen as the only alternative. Tension between the various cultural groups is endemic, hate crime is common, a sense of isolationism is pervasive. Crime rates are up, there are few public recreation facilities for young people, school dropout rates are serious. Yes, life within this community is grim and seems to hold little prospect for a secure and stable future, what many others—those before Ground Zero for example—had come to expect as their birthright.

Within this context, a theatre troupe has been commissioned to help the community begin a conversation about what is possible and what is not. Funds are being directed to support dialogue and to activate community members to converse with each other and problem solve what, if anything, they can do to directly intervene in healing the dislocation, especially for the young people. The task for this particular troupe is a challenge: to create participatory theatre forms in which youth and adults can begin to process how they feel about the world in which they live and, further, to interrogate what is possible for them to change in their lives; what is not; and how they can build a community together that is not powered by fractured, violent, and oppressive encounters.

HOW APPLIED THEATRE HELPS COMMUNITIES PROCESS ISSUES

The work of the communities who embrace theatre as a necessary imperative to transform human behavior is the focus of this book. I am likening this work to an applied theatre—a theatre that is not simply a presentational medium that occurs within a conventional mainstream theatre house. This is a theatre that is taken out into nontheatrical settings, community centers, parks and streets, prison and rehabilitation venues, therapy and health care sites, housing projects, support service settings, and other locations for the purpose of helping the audience, or the participants, grapple with an issue, event, or question of immediate public and personal concern.

It is an applied theatre because the art form becomes a transformative agent that places the audience or participants in direct and immediate situations where they can witness, confront, and deconstruct aspects of their own and others' actions. Applied theatre is committed to the power of the aesthetic form for raising awareness about how we are situated in this world and what we as individuals and as communities might do to make the world a better place.

APPLIED THEATRE HEIGHTENS AWARENESS

The applied theatre is powered by a need to change: a community is hurting and theatre can enable people to process their hurt; or if there are too many unnecessary acts of disease, of hate, and of substance abuse in our midst, theatre might be one way for a community to consider alternatives. Applied theatre opens up new perspectives, poses options, and anticipates change.

The term *applied theatre* has been gathering increasing momentum in recent years. Institutions of higher learning around the world, but most especially in Australia, England, and the United States, have simultaneously designed applied theatre degree programs and research centers dedicated to investigating this question: How can theatre be harnessed in nontheatrical settings to build stronger communities?

Applied theatre became a particularly useful description given that it encompasses the breadth of work that theatre programs were creating inside and outside of educational settings, mostly in nontheatrical environments for diverse purposes—raising awareness, posing alternatives, healing psychological wounds or barriers, challenging contemporary discourses, voicing the views of the silent and marginal. The following five brief descriptions highlight this diversity.

Raising Awareness

During this twenty-first century, HIV continues to plague the globe and is especially rampant in what we sometimes call third-world countries. In these communities, it is difficult to find the means to educate people about safe-sex practices or to help raise awareness about AIDS and how it can be prevented. In what is now widely referred to as the theatre for development (TfD) movement, many troupes have been commissioned, or driven, to create participatory theatre works in which information concerning life-and-death issues can be relayed effectively. Drawing on the traditions of storytelling and narrative discourses, troupes engage in theatre as the principal way to heighten understanding of AIDS, HIV, and safe sex.

In other settings, informally staged street performances become important events for calling attention to unjust political policies such as those that actively promote exclusion of certain cultural groups, or budgetary reductions in fiscal affairs such as cuts to arts organizations and/or social and health services. Invisible or legislative theatre is but one response to this movement: Events are staged without audiences necessarily knowing that they are witnessing a theatrical moment. A theatre program focused on government cutbacks in health services to minorities might be staged in public centers like shopping malls, trains, libraries, churches.

Here actors might create a lively exchange between a government official and an individual directly affected by the cutback. The actors attempt to engage the audience, the observers, in the exchange. The actors raise the issue and canvass the varied positions, highlighting how the proposed cutback will adversely impact a given population. The audience is unaware until the end of the presentation that they are watching a fictional event. The program is motivated by activism and the need to address issues of discrimination, inequity, and isolation.

Posing Alternatives

In a coastal town where the sun and beaches are features in promotional materials, there is a large young male population disaffected from school, their families, their community, themselves. A health services department in this town is at a loss to know what to do to help these young men. A theatre company is asked to create an applied theatre project whereby positive role models are presented and examined. The intention of the applied theatre is to help social workers find and examine strategies for effectively dealing with people in a certain situation. The company creates the following scenario:

> Mel is fifteen years old, the oldest male in his family now that his father has left home. He has a younger sister who looks up to him, yet she is a source of annoyance to Mel. His mother is not coping well as a single parent. She barely manages to pay the bills and takes her anxieties out on her son. Mel is losing interest in school and his friends, he begins raiding his mother's liquor cabinet. There are suggestions that he might cause himself physical harm if this pattern continues.

The scenario is presented to the social workers, whom I'll refer to as the participants. They consider how Mel is adapting to his changed life circumstances and whether he has alternatives to the dangerous self-destructive pathway he seems to be on. The workers are presented with situations from Mel's life to provide some context as to how he is interacting with his world. The participants hotseat Mel, play out situations that might occur between him and a social worker, and examine them. Do the social workers questions seem appropriate? How is Mel responding during the encounter? How might we change this encounter so that the social worker could be more supportive? The role-play becomes a vehicle for dialogue among the social workers. They consider issues related to language, nuance, gesture, and how important these are when faced by young people in Mel's situation.

This scenario becomes an applied theatre project aimed at enabling social workers to consider the variety of alternatives and options at their disposal as they interact with Mel. He becomes a representative of those young people in varying states of crisis or alienation. The situation is a delicate one that requires tact and sensitivity. The participants in this program seek strategies for helping young people like Mel. Through the role-play, Mel becomes the catalyst, the protagonist, for exploring issues focused on identity, acceptance, and marginalization.

Increasing numbers of this type of project are being sponsored by health, housing, and rehabilitation departments—departments that are more interested in the power of theatre as a resource for social welfare workers, youth detainment officers, counselors, and others interested in communities' capacity to effect change in the lives of people who seem out of sync with themselves and their world.

Healing Psychological Wounds or Barriers

A group of fifth graders (10- to 11-year-olds) witness a major terrorist catastrophe from their classroom window, the sudden collapse of the Twin Towers at the World Trade Center in New York City. A drama therapist is commissioned to work with these children over some weeks to help them share their stories and fears as a result of witnessing this event firsthand. Through the conversations and role-plays between the children and the therapist, they create a play based on their words and thoughts—a theatre event that helps them examine their anxieties.

Although this event involves a public presentation for parents and members of the school community, for the therapist, this presentational aspect is less important than the process of the children articulating what they saw on that terrible day. The nonpresentational aspect of the therapist's work—how children use theatre to share the way they are coping now and to express their challenges as they begin to rebuild the school community—is the priority.

Nonetheless, in the discussion following the presentation, parents, members of the wider community, and audience members commented on how the conversations and role-plays provided some relief and release from their anxieties. It was a healing process for this audience to observe this work and share their stories.

This project has the characteristics of applied theatre; work of this nature can have a therapeutic quality, which aims to rebuild a fracture, a scarring. Applied theatre is now part of the armor of those professions concerned with processing trauma, grief, and loss. For instance, there is an established drama therapy movement concerned with using theatre strategies to help individuals and groups deal with a range of personal dislocations from society. In a society where there is a frightening occurrence of child sex crime, youth prostitution, gang rape, and other shocking abuses of power and privilege, theatre can be applied in the "rebuilding" and healing of those in need. In addition, applied theatre has been used in marriage therapy, with fractured parent–child relationships, and for other complex issues that generate a range of emotional and psychological stresses. We are seeing an increasing use of applied theatre in prisons, encounter groups, alcohol and drug abuse centers, and retreats of all kinds, including social and business settings.

Challenging Contemporary Discourses

A shocking hate crime occurs in a quiet remote country center, the brutal beating of gay, twenty-one-year-old Matthew Shepard by two local young men. A director and playwright are struck by this event and wonder whether this crime and the attitudes that motivated it are representational of a larger public trend. The circumstances surrounding this particular attack are especially troublesome. The two men who murdered Shepard engaged Matthew in a friendly conversation in a bar, then left with him in their pickup truck. They drove Shepard to a remote location, dragged him from the vehicle, tied him to a fence, and proceeded to kick and bludgeon him to death. From their first meeting, it seems their intention was to kill him because he was openly gay. Their friendliness in the bar was a scam and lure to get him into their truck. The murderers act out a role of friends so that they can entice the unknowing victim to his execution.

"Look like th' innocent flower," exclaims Lady Macbeth, "but be the serpent under 't" (Shakespeare 1963, I.v:66–67). Just as Lady Macbeth urges her husband to act out a loyal role with King Duncan while secretly plotting to kill him, the history of humankind, it seems, is replete with such duplicitous acts. The Nazis who played music as their captors were led to gas chambers; the pedophiles who seduced young boys with gifts and other supposed acts of goodness; the fanatics who enter bars and restaurants on the pretense of seeking entertainment while having strapped dynamite around their chests. The world of make-believe can be powered by a deadly sense of purpose.

What motivates hate? How can people commit such horrible crimes? How is it possible for the brutal beating of people like Matthew Shepard and others to occur? Applied theatre is but one forum where these issues can be raised and considered. In the Shepard example, the playwright contemplates whether theatre can play a role in exploring what leads to hate such as those attacks fueled by homophobia. He joins all of those artists concerned with probing why injustices and oppressions occur. How might theatre open up a dialogue about why certain groups in society feel privileged and superior? What leads humanity to want to segregate and annihilate? What is there about the human spirit that wants to build a future through opposition and difference?

In the case of Shepard, a dramatist applied the theatre form to critique contemporary mainstream discourses, discourses often powered by oppression of minorities and those who live in the margins. He visited and interviewed residents of the community where the hate crime took place and generated a theatre text based on the interviews, which demonstrated a complex range of viewpoints about Shepard and his lifestyle. The narratives exposed through these interviews were rendered into a dramatic text that was performed in a number of locations, including the city where the crime happened. When presented, it generates considerable conversation about the kind of world in which we live and want to create. Applied theatre provides a significant public service by enabling communities to talk freely about their own, and others', perceptions and values.[1]

Voicing the Views of the Silent and Marginal

As part of the activities during Domestic Violence Week in a small rural town, an applied theatre work is designed for women, who may or may not be victims, living in a community and housing project where there has been an alarming rise in reports of domestic violence. The government department responsible for administering the housing project has decided that a theatre project focused on domestic violence could be an important supplement to its activities. A theatre group has been asked to create a participatory program so that women can begin to process how a community might deal with this issue—if women experience domestic violence, what options do they have in their home environment?

Following a field trip to the housing project, the theatre workers wrote a scene between two characters—Man and Woman—which suggested that Woman is a silent victim of a gradual escalation of vicious incidents of beating by her male partner. This scene hints at many of the questions victims/survivors of domestic violence raised to the theatre workers during their field trip: How can women remove themselves from violent situations when they are so dependent on their partners? What steps can be taken to prevent physical and verbal attacks in the home? Why do the perpetrators of domestic violence need to control the victims/survivors? The scene between Man and Woman would serve as the basis for a series of participatory activities in which the audience could investigate the options open to the domestic violence victim/survivor.

The female audience is provided with opportunities to hotseat the woman protagonist by going into the role of her friend or confidant, providing advice and grappling with the contradictions and ambiguities of her life: What are the dilemmas that Woman faces? What choices does she really have in this situation? Through their various interventions, the audience members begin a dialogue on what life choices are available for women in crisis situations. They debate the merits of a particular strategy or approach that

---

[1]The playwright referred to here is Moisés Kaufman and the text is "The Laramie Project."

victims/survivors of domestic violence might pursue. The implications of these strategies are examined by the audience.

This applied theatre project generates a fruitful inquiry into what happens when domestic violence is experienced in the home. It aims to place participants within a dramatic situation where they must speak up and be counted. At the close of this particular program, educational help and guidance materials are available for those who want to find out more about the subject. The applied theatre project is sustained by a belief that theatre can be an important tool to enable victims/survivors to voice their views. The marginalized can be heard, but they need assistance when considering their life options.

In each of the examples here, it is the application of the theatrical art form that is being harnessed to help communities determine some aspect of who they are and what they aspire to become. Whether these applications are aimed at facilitating a dialogue, healing a pain, or processing a specific issue of significant importance within a community, theatre is a platform that empowers a transformation. This book examines how this transformation occurs and especially how the art form, particularly the theatrical uses of time, space, and action, can launch participants into virtual worlds where they can experience and interrogate what is possible and what is not within the confines of one's life project. The following paragraphs summarize each chapter.

Chapter One, *Applied Theatre as a Transformative Agent*, introduces readers to how theatre has been and/or can be engaged as a change agent. The expression *change agent* is being used quite deliberately to highlight how theatrical forms can empower people and societies to investigate the problematic nature of the world in which they live and the possible worlds they might inhabit. Like the educational inquiry action researcher whose work is driven by a premise that all is not well in the world, the applied theatre worker is either commissioned to or interested in creating theatre that raises issues and questions that need to be addressed: How might theatre help a community address the issue of safe-sex practices? What role might theatre have in improving children's literacy levels or comprehension of curriculum concepts? The realization that theatre can be a potent transformative agent and that it can open our eyes to new ways of seeing and understanding is a central theme of this chapter.

Chapter Two, *Implementing Applied Theatre*, highlights the conditions required when introducing applied theatre to a range of communities. Drawing on participatory forms of theatre, the chapter argues that the central elements required for applied theatre to be successful are people, passion, and a platform—the three *p*s. Further illustrations of how the three *p*s work are provided. We also examine how applied theatre renders change in the community. The chapter examines the notion of praxis—an applied theatre praxis—where teaching artists work in collaboration with communities so that they can jointly render a dialogue about change and transformation. The implementation challenges of an applied theatre are outlined and the compromises these challenges sometimes force are examined.

Chapter Three, *The Applied Theatre Teaching Artist*, investigates the various stances leaders and facilitators of applied theatre need to assume. The term *teaching artist* is gaining increasing recognition as an apt description of the dual roles of artist and educator that encompasses the work in the applied theatre. Teaching artists need to be open to reading field context and should be able to change their plans at any given moment. There was a time when the teaching artist led participants through a sequence of presentations and activities, seemingly bearing no resemblance to one another. Outcomes were predicted in advance; set programs, which wouldn't vary, were established; and participants were provided with few, if any, opportunities to negotiate the work in progress. This chapter deconstructs the particular skills teaching artists need to develop. It pinpoints some of the dangers imbedded in a praxis that fails to include the voices of the participants as programs are designed and implemented.

Chapter Four, *The Ethics of Applied Theatre*, highlights the challenges applied theatre places on teaching artists as programs are researched and devised. What ethical demands does the applied theatre place on those who commission the work, those who design it, those who experience it? Because applied theatre is often grounded in the stories and experiences of people, what special authorizations are required to protect confidentiality of participants as they share their life histories? Can applied theatre use actual material as the basis for investigations or should the material be disguised? The content of many applied theatre programs needs to be sensitively handled and facilitators need to have a strong hold on group dynamics and be able to change the direction of work when it seems that responses might become too heated and/or too personalized.

This chapter examines the responsibilities of applied theatre teaching artists who must tread very cautiously as they search for the most appropriate strategies to open up a dialogue on a range of topics. Teaching artists should not see themselves as the experts with the solutions to life's complex and bewildering questions; such an authoritative stance can sometimes stymie participation. The applied theatre engages participants in an important conversation on issues directly experienced in the community. How teaching artists handle these issues, and the ethical obligations they must commit to, are explored in this chapter.

Chapter Five, *Evaluating Applied Theatre*, examines issues related to the successful implementation of the applied theatre. For programs to be successful in the community, the applied theatre worker needs to be able to monitor whether objectives and aims are being met. Data on how participants are engaging with the work needs to be gathered: How is the applied theatre program opening up a dialogue? What strategies most ably facilitate that dialogue? What do participants say about their applied theatre experience? What advice can the participants provide about the structure of the applied theatre, and how might that structure be strengthened? These questions point to a need to reflect on the quality of applied theatre programs.

Evaluations might take different forms depending on who the evaluation is meant for. A commissioning agent, for example, might be looking for a certain kind of evidence as to a program's success, and this evidence may need to be presented in an accessible and ready form. The teaching artists could be looking for a different kind of evidence—evidence to do with the effective design of the program—and the extent to which their own questioning and facilitation enabled participants to engage in the manner that was envisaged. This chapter explores the methods by which data can be collected and places a responsibility on teaching artists to be reflective practitioners as they go about data collection and analysis.

Applied Theatre introduces readers to the rich possibilities that the theatre form presents for a range of communities as they grapple with issues related to identity; social change; human development and healing; and what it means to live together during difficult, uncertain, and even stressful times. The theatre is an applied art form because it is through, and in, the theatrical experience that these issues can be most immediately addressed. Rather than talk about the issues, participants experience them firsthand as they encounter fictional and sometimes real characters who grapple with what it means to live in this new century.

The theatre is *applied* because it is taken out from the conventional mainstream theatre house into various settings in communities where many members have no real experience in theatre form. The theatre becomes a medium for action, for reflection but, most important, for transformation—a theatre in which new modes of being can be encountered and new possibilities for humankind can be imagined.

It is my hope that readers, who have had little or no experience with the power of the theatre form to construct new, alternative, and evolving narratives, will find the examples in this book insightful and helpful to their own understanding as they begin to further contemplate the role that applied theatre might have in their own and others' lives.

1

APPLIED THEATRE AS A TRANSFORMATIVE AGENT

Applied theatre operates from a recognition that throughout time theatre has been applied or rendered as a powerful educative tool. The here and now of a theatre event immediately entraps audiences within an experience, and if managed well, the theatre performance can empower audience members to act as commentators to what is being played out in front of them. Many would argue that good theatre always aims to entrap participants like this, providing audience members with experiences that shatter familiar perspectives and open up new possibilities for conceptualizing the world in which they live. This attitude is common, and we could all cite examples of theatre experiences that have had this desired effect. But the applied theatre takes the art form to nontheatrical settings where audiences or participants often have no experience or interest in theatre.

The applied theatre operates from a central transformative principle: to raise awareness on a particular issue (safe-sex practices), to teach a particular concept (literacy and numeracy), to interrogate human actions (hate crimes, race relations), to prevent life-threatening behaviors (domestic violence, youth suicide), to heal fractured identities (sexual abuse, body image), to change states of oppression (personal victimization, political disenfranchisement). This transformative principle shares much with other participatory and community theatre movements, where a central emphasis is on the applications of theatre to help people reflect more critically on the kind of society in which they live.

The theatre in education (TIE) movement is one example of how theatre has been applied in educational settings to address issues. Here, participants are presented with challenging scenarios through which they can find ways of using the theatre form to resolve the dilemmas the scenarios present. This work is sometimes described as *participatory theatre* because audience members are often required to enter the fictitious world of the drama, by role-playing or hotseating[1] characters and by engaging with other strategies that permit them to reflect carefully on the subject matter being focused on.

Community and popular theatre are other examples of applications of theatre to help individuals and groups make statements about who they are and what they aspire to become. These movements can have a political imperative to them, such as those found in radical street theatre, theatre of the oppressed, and theatre for change. The interest in the power of theatre to shift human consciousness, to unite disempowered communities, to activate for significant transformation in the workplace and other settings is what characterizes this theatre.

Theatre has been used quite successfully in developing countries to explore ways third-world societies can more fully consider how to improve the quality of their own and others' lives. The theatre for development (TfD) movement shares much with the applied theatre: both are concerned with building knowledge, both are interested in layering participatory strategies in which audiences can begin to experience directly some of the challenges the work raises. According to Ahmed (2002):

> Issues commonly dealt with in these plays are social injustice, dowry, polygamy, *fatwa*, arbitrary divorce, gender discrimination, illiteracy, unjust possession of public resources by the power cliques, superstitious health practices, degradation of the environment and its consequences, and the positive impact of various development actions on the lives of the people. (211)

Applied theatre though is not necessarily an event that takes place solely in targeted third-world communities where there are

---

[1]*Hotseating* is a strategy often used in applied theatre to assist groups in constructing a dialogue around the questions being investigated; in this chapter, what are the factors that shape youth alienation? How might our interventions transform states of alienation, depression, a sense of being the outsider?

alarming concerns about health, literacy, and political issues. The TfD movement has its own histories and emphases, often related to raising living standards and overthrowing political oligarchies (Byam 1999). This work can sometimes occurs in war-zone territories where groups are fighting to occupy land and to annihilate one's perceived enemy.

In this book's introduction, we have seen how notions of a war zone have been radically reconceptualized since September 11, 2001, after the bombing of the New York City Twin Towers. Here, a community relatively distant from the war zones of Bosnia and Israel experiences firsthand the hate of terrorism—the willful desire to obliterate humankind. Applied theatre artists do not conceive of their mission as one belonging solely to a third world or powered by those aims of the TfD movement. Applied theatre workers are driven by a desire to provide insight, to interrogate understandings of community, and to contemplate notions of the better, the just.

It doesn't matter whether this is theatre artists attempting to achieve cross-cultural dialogue between Palestinian and Israeli cultures, or between the Maori and Pakeha cultures in New Zealand; or a kindergarten teacher in Brooklyn, New York, struggling to have her five-year-olds understand that stealing other people's possessions is wrong and wanting to create a theatre program to help the children explore the issue. In each instance, there is a shared mission to apply the theatre form as an aesthetic event to activate human consciousness in unique ways (Greenwood 2001, 193; Taylor 2000).

It is evident that the applied theatre operates from a driving mission to deeply probe some aspect of the world in which we live, and, sometimes, this mission might have a political orientation to it. This is one reason why the South American theatre director Augusto Boal has been an influential writer on the evolution of the applied theatre. Boal (1985) argues that at its most effective, theatre places audiences on both the inside and the outside of a virtual world, and it is this duality that leads to significant reflective experiences. Audience members are having an experience of an event while controlling the nature of the experience they are having. They engage in a form of internal dialogue in which they critique the experience at the very same moment they submit to that experience.

In a stealing example, kindergarten children reenact a shopping expedition where children plan for a birthday party. They imagine buying candy, streamers, and presents. While on the expedition, the children find a doll and decide they will steal it. Later, they are confronted by the little girl who lost the doll, played by the teacher. In role, the teacher wonders whether the children have seen the doll her mother gave to her for her birthday. The kindergarteners are trapped within the imaginary event and immediately probe the morality of their decision to steal the toy. The children must try to understand their actions in the drama and to articulate how they would feel if their doll had been stolen by someone else. Their actions in and out of the drama provide the catalyst for a contemplative discussion.

Here's another example. During a therapy session, Michael, a twenty-seven-year-old gay male who has trouble accepting his sexuality, retells the many abuses inflicted by his father. Through structured directions, the therapist requests Michael to enact various imaginary and real roles, which leads to many agonizing insights as well as to his self-fulfilling journey from victim to survivor. The therapist's need to shepherd Michael's transformation from a state of distress to a fulfilling one has much in common with the applied theatre artist's drive to help participants work through difficult challenges in positive and fulfilling ways (Landy 1993, 110).

THE PARTICIPANT–OBSERVER

Applied theatre pivots on a conviction that theatre form can uniquely place individuals in situations where they can interrogate some issue, confront a problem, and analyze their own relationship to the world in which they live. There is a commitment to having audience members observe a theatre presentation, or scenario, and also participate in it. This can be extremely challenging work and raises numerous ethical issues, as James Thompson has identified in his work about the war-torn territory of Sri Lanka. He wonders about the responsibility of the applied theatre artist in areas where "dependency, alcoholism, education and typhoid" are ripping communities apart (2002, 110).

What ethical responsibilities do applied theatre workers experience when they are in these zones? Should applied theatre be presenting a range of issues the downtrodden and the exploited can both participate in *and* observe? Although applied theatre can become a useful way for communities in crisis to express concerns about what is preventing them from reaching their aspirations, can outside interventionists really share in the grief and devastation of these communities? What role does theatre have in a time of widespread conflict? These are some excellent questions about the purposes and intent of applied theatre. When we talk about a transformative theatre, whose transformations are being promoted and valued?

The challenge of a transformative theatre is certainly apparent when we investigate work that demands a huge emotional investment from the participants. In the preceding therapy example, we have evidence of participants being invited to directly relive moments of great and deep pain from their past. The therapist has a strong commitment to emotional attachment and believes that sometimes the best way to get on the inside of a past event is to locate its essential narrative details and recreate them, with the participant/client reenacting numerous fictitious and real roles.

In a different setting that focused on the rehabilitation of offenders, an aspect of the counseling process can involve having the incarcerated recreate the moments when they committed their crimes. Thompson wonders about the morality of having criminals relive offenses in this way. After witnessing numerous sessions in which criminals reenact their crimes, he wonders what possible merit reenactments have in a rehabilitation process. "The lead participant in all sessions I saw was emotionally distraught," he writes, "and 'out of control' by the end of the session" (Thompson 1998, 19). The ethical dimensions present during a process of participant–observation are the focus of Chapter 4.

In the applied theatre, we are not so much interested in having participants surrender their capacity to think and to reflect on the nature of the experience they are having. Applied theatre works best when participants are actively engaged in critically exploring the implications of their own and others' actions. This dual stance—the willingness to both participate in the work and to understand the nature of the participation—might usefully be described as *participant–observation*. The participant–observer, a stance familiar in various qualitative modes of research, highlights the two frames of being and not being. The applied theatre creates situations where participants submit to and control the nature of the experience they are having, a phenomenon Boal likens to metaxis. The state of *metaxis* is achieved when a dialogue occurs between the real and the fictional worlds. As Boal (1985, 104) argues, the spectators must not leave "their brains with their hats upon entering the theatre, as do bourgeois spectators." The capacity of the spectators to become spect-actors—where they consciously and deliberately reflect and act on the implications of their own and others' actions—is central to an applied theatre. The spectators are not merely experiencing they are actively contemplating and critiquing the nature of their experiencing.

In many respects, this stance closely mirrors what British educator Gavin Bolton (1979, 21) referred to as "thought in action." While commenting on structured, improvisatory events that occur in classroom drama, Bolton's theory of drama in education holds much currency for an applied theatre. Bolton has examined the history of much classroom activity in drama and found it to be dependent on participants' submission and willingness to reenact or mimic events in a linear fashion. Rather than collapsing events into focused moments subject to scrutiny and virtual forensic examination, many drama educators have argued that interrogation gets in the way of the experience. Like Boal, Bolton argues for theatre praxis in which transformation is key to the participants' experience. "I am making it happen, it is happening to me" neatly summarizes the dual nature of the activity that takes place within those who participate in the applied theatre. Participants are having an experience while simultaneously understanding the nature of the experience they are having.

When applied theatre operates well, it can challenge audience members, spectators, to ask themselves the questions: What might I do if I were placed in the same circumstance? How does the experience being demonstrated in front of me relate to my own life circumstances? To what extent can I learn from the experience? How might my life be changed or transformed? Of course, not all theatre encounters achieve these states of recognition, or transformation, and we can think of moments in the theatre when we have merely been entertained and not challenged to rethink a familiar issue or contemplate a previously unthought-of idea.

Many theatre critics have criticized those theatre forms in which audience members are rendered numb from their spectatorship—that is, virtually hypnotized into nonthinking states. Both Boal and Bolton have been influenced considerably by the praxis of Bertolt Brecht, the influential German playwright, director, and dramaturg. Brecht was especially critical of those forms of theatre in which audiences are cast into virtual somnambulist states, as noted in the following (Willett 1977):

> True their eyes are open, but they stare rather than see, just as they listen rather than hear. They look at the stage as if in a trance—an expression which comes from the Middle Ages, the days of witches and priests. Seeing and hearing are activities, and can be pleasant ones, but these people seem relieved of any activity and like men to whom something is being done. This detached state, where they seem to give over to vague but profound sensations, grows deeper the better the work of the actors. (166)

Writing in 1948, Brecht was arguing against a particular kind of German tradition where audience submission and identification were dominant traits. Too strong an emotional state might release audience members into the world of the theatre without having their critical faculties raised to a point at which they can critique and respond in a metacognitive fashion. Brecht's new theatre would appeal less to spectators' feelings than to their ability to reason—to understand what powers their own place in the world.

Observation is critical to one's participation, just as participation is powered by one's perspective or observation of the work. If transformation is to occur in participants, opportunities to reflect on their actions need to be weaved into the applied theatre. The example in the next section should clarify this transformative power.

WIDE-AWAKENESS: CREATING MOMENTS OF CHANGE IN THE COMMUNITY

I would like to begin by deconstructing an applied theatre project powered at every phase of its genesis by notions of transformation. Transformation does not happen in a vacuum, it requires the deliberate structuring of strategies that facilitate a "wide-awakeness" in participants.

The distinguished philosopher, critic, and social commentator, Maxine Greene, claims that aesthetic experiences are at their most resonant when they open up participants to the different possibilities in which their lives might be realized. "I am trying to awaken young persons and their teachers to loving the questions," she argues, "to wondering, to refusing the crusts of convention, to an awareness of what is not yet."

This state of *wide-awakeness*, a heightened consciousness, is at the heart of her aesthetic education. "And always it is an effort to open new spaces in consciousness, to break with confinement in square rooms" (Greene 1999, 15). Such wide-awake states might offer humanity a break from the routine of drudge, from a world where young people in particular might be presented with more hopeful and positive images of themselves and their society.

Throughout time many teaching artists have been keen to explore how theatre can be a transformative agent. I have already referred to three influential practitioners—Brecht, Boal, and Bolton. In recent times, we have seen new artists emerge, such as Cohen-Cruz (1998) and Rodd (1998), who are equally concerned with how theatre can facilitate important dialogues on culture and identity, issues often focusing on power, authority, and community change. There will be many others whose praxis will serve as a backdrop to this text. What these artists share is a desire to engage the theatre form for the purposes of bringing forward a conversation; that conversation can most usefully occur when participants are challenged to *make* theatre rather than to watch it.

We should imagine that the following project was commissioned by a statewide health department for the purposes of intervention and transformation in the lives of young people. I will name the project *Mel: Society at Risk*, isolate how it was structured, and describe what the key issues were for the teaching artists who created it. This project demonstrates many of the defining features of applied theatre and will reinforce the principles of praxis that inform this text—the formative work of the Brazilian, Paulo Freire, who argued that at the heart of educational transformation is an enabling of human beings to consciously reflect on their actions and then change their behavior in light of their discoveries.[2] Such transformation is a praxis: action–reflection–transformation.

◆ AN APPLIED THEATRE PROJECT— MEL: A SOCIETY AT RISK

The Context

Let us imagine that an agency responsible for administering matters pertaining to public health has been increasingly concerned by the staggering growth in teenage suicides. Alarming statistics reveal there has been a threefold increase in youth suicide in the last thirty years; suicide is the most common cause of death among men under thirty and 10 percent of young people living in certain areas the agency has administrative responsibility for attempt suicide at least once. Increased funds have been allocated to help communities construct a dialogue about ways of combating the trends identified by these statistics. Theatre projects that deal with the plight of young people are commissioned and presented in a range of community settings. Equally, applied theatre projects are created to involve audience members, the participants, in responding to scenarios and enacting situations that present different outcomes from those demonstrated by the artists.

The scenario—a dramatic situation created by the teaching artist—serves as the catalyst for the target audience's participation. This fictitious agency was especially interested in a project targeted for counselors, therapists, and social workers who need to deal

---

[2]Freire's work (1970) is examined further in my earlier book, *The Drama Classroom* (Taylor 2000).

[3]Theatre in education is loaded with a particular cultural history; the term connotes a specific way of working pioneered in England in the 1960s. Teams of actor–teachers create participatory issue-based theatre work and tour this work in British schools. The programs are usually structured around a dramatic actor–teacher presentation, which is then "problem solved" by the audience. Often the audience assumes roles and enacts situations. This work has been quite influential, despite the fact that many British teams had their funding slashed during the 1980s and 1990s. For further information on this work, consult Jackson (1993).

directly with young people labeled "at-risk." Although there have been any number of conventional TIE[3] teams, which tour schools and focus on young people in crisis, few have been developed especially for those adults who have responsibility for implementing support services.

The intention of the program described here was to construct a dialogue with these authoritative figures about the quality of their advice to *at-risk* young people and to process the effectiveness of strategies commonly applied to such youth. Together this target audience would productively process the circumstances that might lead to self-harm and consider what actions they could take to help decrease the incidence of suicide among young people.[4]

Principles for Planning Applied Theatre

1. Applied Theatre Is Thoroughly Researched

The teaching artists working on this project are faced with a number of challenges, including:

- Who is the audience for the applied theatre?
- What does the applied theatre project aim to achieve?
- How can the applied theatre be designed to meet the needs of the audience?

The responses to questions like these are complex and multifaceted.

The audiences, it turns out, are numerous. For example, they could be the adults who are concerned with the welfare of young people, who will directly experience the program, and/or the wider community who might observe it; then there is the agency that commissioned the applied theatre in the first place. Each of these audiences has their own expectations of what the program should achieve.

The first critical aspect of the planning process is to construct a dramatic scenario that will hold resonance for participants. To do this, evidence needs to be solicited on the nature of young people's experiences in the community and why suicide is seen as a necessary outcome for so many. Research demonstrates that one reason why young people feel so alienated from their communities is that

---

[4]The context for this work is supported in Ball (1999).

the school system they are expected to participate in does not actively attempt to listen to them; and reports of alienation from schools are mounting. Although numerous educational studies have spoken of the importance of dialogue, interaction, and genuine encounters between members of the school community, for the most part what is pursued by educators is a monologic encounter in which the voices of participants are filtered and controlled by teachers.[5]

Likewise, in the wider workplace environment, there is constant frustration that intimidation by one's supervisor can shape the quality of discourse, especially when a supervisor is in control of promotion and salary increases. Opportunities for workers to question or criticize a supervisor's approach or stance are thwarted if penalties are foreseen.[6] The challenge then for the applied theatre teaching artist is to create a scenario to provoke significant dialogue from the participants so that they can see that their opinions and viewpoints are able to directly influence the outcome and development of events.

2. Applied Theatre Seeks Incompleteness

The applied theatre here focuses on Mel, whose life appears to be in flux. His father recently left home to pursue a relationship with another male. Mel has a younger sister, Tracey, who is ten. Mel and Tracey now live with their mother. She has expectations for her children, especially Mel, to assume more responsibility around the house. It is unclear what kind of financial support Mel's father is going to pay because he has left without any clear indication of a plan for interacting with this family in the future. A team of four teaching artists are required for the *Mel: Society at Risk* scenario[7]:

Actor One: The facilitator who introduces the work to the audience and leads the participants through the range of strategies

---

[5]For examples of this evidence, consult Taylor (1998).

[6]For details about this, see Smigiel (1996).

[7]The work is partly informed by projects I implemented through the Centre for Applied Theatre Research at Griffith University in Australia, where I was director from 1998 to 2001. I am grateful to the following teaching artists for their dedication to this work: Steve Ball, Mark Stanley, Erin Mulvey, Meryl Simpson, Adam Tucker, Gabrielle Tully, and Carol McGiffin.

Actor Two: Mel, who recently turned fifteen, is missing
Actor Three: Assumes two roles—Tracey, Mel's ten-year-old
   sister, and Chris, Mel's fifteen-year-old male best friend
Actor Four: Assumes two roles—Mel's mother; Sam, Mel's
   fifteen-year-old long-time female best friend

The project begins with the facilitator explaining to the audience (from now on, referred to as the *participants*) that what they each share is a desire to protect and advance the interests of young people. Sometimes situations they are placed in are difficult ones, and it is not always possible to know whether the advice they provide to young people who seek their support is correct.

The participants are presented with a challenging scenario concerning the well-being of the fifteen-year-old male, Mel. They are instructed to endeavor to respond to this case in a way that is logical for them. Further, all the participants must imagine they are teachers in Mel's school, and they should not be burdened by specific questions about the nature of the school—for example, whether it is coeducational, rural, and/or places a lot of emphasis on sports. These matters may or may not become apparent as the scenario develops. The text, to a certain extent, is incomplete, which enables the participants to construct their own "reading" of the events. The facilitator asks participants to create the environment of a faculty meeting room, perhaps suggesting that they put two rows of chairs in a semicircular formation and then stand behind the chairs. When they sit on their chairs, they are "enrolled" as the teachers in Mel's school. The facilitator, sitting in front of the rows of chairs, assumes the role of the school counselor, then (in role) says:

School Counselor: As you know, the principal has asked me to fill you in on the details concerning the events of today. I realize that the hour is late but we appreciate you staying on after the school day has finished. The police are currently interviewing the principal and they indicated to me that they would like to come and speak with you after that meeting. The details of Mel's disappearance are as follows:

- Mel was present for the morning attendance register and went to his first three classes—social studies, information technology, and gym.

- His school friends, Chris and Sam, say that he left gym immediately after the session finished and was seen running. Given it was then a twenty-minute recess, they thought he was going to the school cafeteria. By the time they got there about 10:40 AM, they could not find him. When Mel did not show for his math class, Chris was concerned but not too panicked. However, the janitor came to the class and said that a schoolbag belonging to Mel had been found in the gym locker room.
- When the three friends were supposed to attend a drama rehearsal at lunch time and he wasn't there, they came to me as Mel's school counselor and I raised the alarm. His mother has no idea where he is but said he has been acting strange since his father moved out of the house.
- The police are now here. This is all the information available at present.

As the school counselor, the facilitator fields a few questions from the teachers. The emphasis though is on the facilitator baiting participant interest by raising more questions than providing solutions, by throwing the responsibility on the teachers to problem solve what might have happened, and by working toward incompleteness. This role-play ends with the facilitator stating that the police are at the door wanting to meet with the teachers. They clearly want to brief the teachers on the latest developments. They are carrying Mel's schoolbag.

3. Applied Theatre Demonstrates Possible Narratives

The facilitator narrates the following:

The police inform the teachers that following extensive interviews with his mother, sister, and friends, a picture of Mel's life as a fifteen-year-old is emerging. Contained within this picture are insights into Mel's relationship with his family, his friends, and himself.

The facilitator explains that this picture will now be demonstrated by a reenactment. In other words, instead of hearing the narrative of Mel's life, they will "see" the narrative through three vignettes. The vignettes here demonstrate aspects of Mel's school life, home life, and life with his friends.

Vignette One: After School

Mel's home, lying on floor pondering his school report. Musical background features material Mel, a fifteen-year-old popular student, might listen to.

Chris: *(entering)* Mel, guess what? I am on the cross-country team. I can't believe it. How come you didn't try out? You're one of the best athletes in school.

Mel: Not interested.

Chris: But you do it every year.

Mel: Yeah, but not this year, okay!

Sam: *(enters running with new computer game)* Hey, hey, hey. Level 10 Lawn Mower Rider. You've never got there before Mel.

Chris: Sam, guess what? I got into the cross-country team.

Sam: Wow, you and Mel, what a team.

Mel: I'm not doing it this year.

Sam: But you do it every year.

Mel: I can't this year, too much work and stuff.

Sam: But you only work two days a week. You can get out of it.

Mel: No, getting out of rosters is very hard now, and besides I don't want to run this year.

Sam: *(noticing the school report in Mel's hand)* What's that?

Chris: Looks like his report card.

Sam: *(grabbing the report from Mel)* A behavior report? What, Mr. Goody Two Shoes who has never had a detention before *(reads on)*. English . . . "Repeated absences frequently affect performance."

Chris: *(grabbing the report from Sam)* Biology . . . "Disappointing result from a student with great promise."

Sam: *(grabbing the report from Chris)* Math, which used to be your best subject . . . "Concentration lapses lead to careless mistakes." What's this all about Mel?

Mel: *(angrily, finally having retrieved the report card)* I don't know. The school is just making me do it. Mom has to sign this.

Sam: *(conciliatory)* Yeah, okay. What will your dad say? *(notices Mel's disdain)* Well, forget about it. Let's go to McDonald's.

Chris: Yeah, come on let's go to the mall.

Mel: No, I can't. I have got work this afternoon.

Sam: Okay, we will catch up with you later on then.

Mel: Yeah, okay.

Chris: I'll catch you at school tomorrow then.

Mel: (*offhand remark*) Yeah, if I go. I've got to find mom. (*looks at the report card*) See you, Chris. See you, Sam. (*Thinks about father. After a few seconds tears up report card.*) Fuck him!

End of vignette. Mel freezes with torn report card in hand. Rap music fades in.

Vignette Two: The Party

Mel's home. Late on a Saturday night. The three friends are lying on the floor watching TV.

Chris: What did your mom say about the report card?

Mel: I didn't show it to her.

Chris: You're such an idiot.

Mel: And you're a brown nose. (*Some play fighting occurs between Mel and Chris.*)

Sam: (*enters with a bottle of vodka and three glasses*) What time will your mom and Tracey be back?

Mel: Hopefully never! (*pours three vodka shots*) I don't know. She has to collect Tracey after she finishes bingo. I think maybe eleven.

Sam: Bingo. Great. Where's Tracey?

Mel: Watching movies at Eliza's. Okay, one each. (*Hands Sam and Chris the vodka shots. They all drink at once, coughing and spluttering. Mel fills the glasses again.*)

Sam: That was revolting.

Mel: Yeah, I know. Again. (*They all drink at once.*) Okay, this time I'll pour it into Chris' mouth (*grabs Chris' glass, fills it again*)

Sam: No, I'll do it. You hold him (*Mel agrees, gives Sam the shot*)

Chris: Why do I have to go first?

Mel: Because! Now hold still. (*Mel holds onto Chris' head while Sam leans over and pours the drink into his mouth.*) Oh, yuk. You dribbled it everywhere.

Chris: (*giving Mel a push*) I did not.

Mel: (*pushing him back*) Yeah, you did. Okay, my turn. Chris does me.

Sam: (*dripping with innuendo*) Chris "does" you?

Chris: Like father, like son!

Mel: Oh, shut up Chris. (*Sam hands Chris another full shot glass. Sam grabs Mel's head as Chris tips the shot into Mel's mouth, spilling it on him.*)

Chris: You spat half of it out.

Mel: (*pushing Chris*) I did not. You missed.

Sam: (*joining Chris in "rubbishing" Mel*) Mel can't handle his alcohol.

Mel: I can too. He just missed. All right, Sam's turn. I'll do Sam.

Sam: So, now you're "doing" me too. (*Chris grabs Sam's head and holds it as Mel pours the shot into her mouth.*) Remember, go slow.

Mel: Yeah, go slow. (*Mel starts slowly but then pours it all into her mouth at once.*) Ha, ha, it came out your nose. (*Sam gives Mel a push as he jumps up.*) Okay. I'm going to get the beers now. (*Mel rushes off to the side, with his back to Chris and Sam, opens up three beer bottles.*)

Sam and Chris continue to laugh on the floor, and following some gentle wrestling, kiss each other, almost accidentally. Silence. Mel enters, notices the embrace.

Mel: Hey, what's going on?

Chris: Nothing.

Mel: Have you two got something going?

Sam: Yeah, as if.

Chris: (*looking straight at Mel*) What if we have?

> *Vignette freezes. Music fades in. Actors playing Chris and Sam now assume the roles of Tracey, Mel's ten-year-old sister and Mel's mother, respectively.*

Vignette Three: The Family

This vignette takes place in Mel's home. There are two chairs side by side facing the participants. Mother is seated on one chair. Tracey sits on the floor in front of both chairs. Mel stands behind the empty chair.

Tracey: Mom and Dad had a big fight last night. I couldn't hear all of it. Dad's moved in with this guy. He has left.

Mother: (*stares blankly*) I can't believe he has left. "I'm moving in with Jansen," he says. Jansen! Some South African man. What the hell am I supposed to do? The laughing stock of the town (*turns on Mel*). You are not your father. I want responsibility from the men in this house.

Mel: It's not my fault he has gone.

Tracey: Yeah, more from you Mel.

Mel: Why is it up to me? Why do I have to do it all?

Mother: Because Tracey's too young.

Mel: So?

Tracey: And. Mom, I've got to go over to Eliza's for netball practice (*appealing to mother*).

Mel: (*notices his mother looking at him*) I can't do it now.

Mother: (*angry*) Take her. She has to go to her game practice. And I've got too much housework here. Now that Dad's gone you, we, are all going to have to make a few sacrifices.

Tracey: Come on Mel, I've got to go. It's only fifteen minutes.

Mel: (*snidely*) Yeah, right, fifteen minutes down the road, then I have to watch your session, then fifteen minutes back.

Mother: (*fed up*) All right already, shut up both of you. I'll take her. Just get out of my hair Mel. (*Mel throws the chair on the floor and leaves.*)

Actors freeze. Music fades in. Facilitator enters.

Facilitator: The three vignettes you have seen demonstrate aspects of Mel's life, which the police officers reported on at the teachers' meeting. Our task now is to try and interrogate what these vignettes reveal about Mel's school life, his home life, and his life with friends.

The vignettes are meant to provide a catalyst for the work to follow. Mel's life demonstrates that he is very much at odds with his school, his family, and to a lesser extent his friends. His failing grades at school could be attributable to a variety of reasons only hinted at in the vignettes. While Mel seemingly gets on well with his two friends, there is some uneasiness especially when a potential physical relationship between Chris and Sam seems evident. His father's new relationship has thrown a cog into the wheel, and it places new responsibilities on Mel, ones that he is not used to and wants to ignore. Clearly, his mother is stressed by the developments and seemingly is not coping.

The applied theatre raises issues to do with future possibilities:

- *Will this family be able to cope with the demands of the father's departure and the pressures of the father's new relationship?*
- *How will Mel cope with the added responsibilities placed on him in the family unit?*
- *To what extent will the evolving relationship with Sam and Chris affect Mel's interactions with his peers?*

These questions are worthy of further consideration.

The three vignettes could be characterized as creative content input from the teaching artists. This input is critical because it provides context for Mel's life and raises many issues for exploration. Applied theatre is powered by the making of possible and evolving futures, and it focuses on a situated present. In this instance, all is not well with Mel's life. This imbalance is fueled by a past happening—his father left home and his departure caused considerable domestic upheaval. The applied theatre moves toward a beckoning and unknown future. We don't know what is going to happen to Mel, but we are committed to seeking interventions that might offer him assistance.

In applied theatre, there is usually a presentation from the actors that dusts in a background, a background holding deep resonance. This presentation is an incomplete text; a jigsaw puzzle, perhaps, which demands input from the participants if the missing pieces are to be found.

The next episode in the applied theatre project processes how the participants (in this instance, counselors/social workers/youth welfare officers) might use Mel as a case study for interrogating what powers their own praxis when helping young people deal positively with the world around them.

4. Applied Theatre Is Task-Oriented

To further process what the vignettes say about Mel, the participants are divided into four equally sized groups. The facilitator explains that contained within Mel's schoolbag are four objects, what will now be referred to as artifacts:

- A birthday card from Mel's father when he recently turned fifteen
- A journal entry from Mel's diary where he speaks of a growing estrangement with his friends
- The school counselor's report summary of Mel's mixed academic and behavioral results
- The lyrics from a song, clearly written in Mel's hand

In their group, the participants select one of the four artifacts to work with. Knowing what they now believe are some of the qualities of Mel's life, the groups' challenge is to create those artifacts. They will design the birthday card, write Mel's journal entry, write the school report summary, and compose the song lyrics.

Once these have been created, the facilitator asks each group to exchange its artifacts with another group's. Each group then studies each artifact; they discuss it among themselves, and consider what it reveals about Mel's relationship:

- With his father
- With his peers
- With his school
- With himself

Each group reports back to all the participants and shares their observations and any conclusions they have reached about Mel plus, their answers to: What issues about Mel does the artifact raise?

The purpose behind having the participants create the artifacts is that they then begin to have control over the execution of the narrative. If this work is to have a satisfactory impact on the participants, they need to project themselves into the life of Mel. They need to experience his struggle and to hear his perspective on life. By constructing the artifacts, the participants are sharing in the narrative—Mel's story becomes their own. When participants in applied theatre believe they own the work, they invest more of themselves in it. The tasks that participants are given become a critical means for building belief and commitment in the applied theatre.

5. Applied Theatre Poses Dilemmas

The participants, who in real life are counselors, therapists, or social workers, are then asked to imagine that a few days following Mel's disappearance he contacts a telephone hotline service for young people in crisis. The "Teen Help Line" employs a range of experienced social workers to work with young people. The participants are told to imagine that they are working for the hotline on the day Mel phones in a distressed state.

The actor playing Mel comes forward, mimics a telephone in his hand, and says:

Mel: Hello, Teen Help Line? Ummm. I'm not sure what to do? I am in a bit of a mess.

The facilitator asks participants to work as a whole group for this activity. The actor playing Mel is asked to repeat the preceding words and the participants are to imagine they receive this phone call at Teen Help Line. They are to jointly offer responses that they might give as the telephone counselor.

The actor playing Mel is now interacting with the whole group and knows that applied theatre works best when participants struggle to find solutions. There are no easy solutions in applied theatre and the group must work together as a community to try to find the best ploy, the most apt phrase, the most appropriate line of questioning that will encourage Mel to open up.

The previous episodes have shown that Mel's life is in a state of upheaval. He is experiencing emotional difficulties at home, at school, and with his friends. To a certain extent, he may feel betrayed by those around him. The world is closing in on Mel and the responses the telephone counselor offers require sensitivity.

Mel is not going to open up to strangers in five minutes. He needs to find his voice, to feel that he trusts the person he is talking with. The actor playing Mel understands that his responses should be brief, incomplete, and lacking in detail—he probably does not want to speak about his problems directly. The facilitator pushes the participants to find strategies to help Mel talk about the world as he is experiencing it. Perhaps asking Mel to share some of his interests might work; maybe the telephone counselor could share a few tales from his or her own life. Movies, games, music, or sports—in fact anything that could lead to a dialogue is the challenge for the participants here as they take turns conversing with Mel.

At the point at which some successful strategies are shared, the participants are divided into pairs, A and B, and sit on the floor back to back.

A: *Role-plays Mel, who calls the Teen Help Line, and says:* Hello, Teen Help Line? Ummm. I'm not sure what to do? I am in a bit of a mess.
B: *Role-plays the telephone counselor who receives the call.*

This activity provides the whole group with an opportunity to directly experience the states of mind shared by Mel and the telephone counselor. For a few minutes, the pairs spontaneously improvise the conversation that takes place. The facilitator then suggests listening in on a few of the conversations. After each conversation, the facilitator asks the participants:

- *What did you notice about this conversation?*
- *What strategies was the telephone counselor using?*
- *To what extent did these strategies seem successful?*

In this episode, the hotseating of Mel becomes a useful means for the participants to problematize the predicament of at-risk young people. They project themselves into the mind-set of Mel and brainstorm why he feels out of sync with the world around him.

The trick for the teaching artist who assumes the hotseat in this exercise is to construct an evolving narrative, not a fixed narrative. The teaching artists must not be the ones who solve the puzzle. The emphasis is on the participants doing the work, to struggle with the contradictions, to tolerate the ambiguity. A danger of putting one of the participants in the hotseat too soon is that she or he may attempt to provide answers too hastily, and their answers might not resonant with how other participants are reading the situation. Good teaching artists know that it is better to keep raising questions during the early phases of applied theatre rather than to shut inquiry down.

6. Applied Theatre Interrogates Futures

The hotseating from the previous episode suggests that Mel's sense of dislocation is tied into what is happening in his home life.

Although he is not living through a scene of conventional domestic violence, his circumstances are having definite negative effects on his self-image and his sense of self-importance. The participants must now interrogate whether Mel had a different option from the one he pursued (i.e., running away from home). Were there alternatives to the scene at home in which he refuses to take Tracey to netball practice? Could Mel have changed anything about how he processed that encounter?

The actors who created *Vignette Three: The Family* are asked to repeat the scene. Following this second presentation, a general discussion emerges, led by the facilitator, which raises the following questions:

- *What is happening here?*
- *Why does Mel feel put upon?*
- *What precipitates his anger?*
- *Is his anger understandable?*
- *What alternatives does Mel have in this vignette?*

The participants are asked to consider whether, at any point, Mel could have said or done something else that might have led to a different outcome other than his anger and departure. The vignette is to be replayed, and drawing on Augusto Boal's (1985) forum theatre technique,[8] the participants are asked to say "Stop" at the point at which they believe a different intervention could have been introduced by Mel.

When a participant stops the action, he is invited to assume the role of Mel and to try out the suggestion. This intervention is demonstrated and the participants consider whether it transformed the vignette. To what extent did Mel's new action influence the responses of others around him? Discussion then occurs around

---

[8]*Forum theatre* has become an increasingly popular strategy in applied theatre because it places the responsibility on the participants to try out actions directly. Instead of sitting around discussing an idea, the participants experiment in action. That action then becomes a source of conversation, a kind of fruitful dialogue among the participants in which they interrogate how the intervention had an impact on others' behavior. Participants brainstorm whether the intervention worked appropriately or had the sought-after outcome. Here, the spectators become *spectactors* in Boal's eyes—they enter the artistic space and try out possibilities.

the appropriateness of the intervention and whether it secured the desired response.

It is both the intervention and the participants' interrogation of the intervention that is a feature of this work. The intervention challenges participants to attempt a resolution in action. Actions, it is said, speak louder than words. It might be very well for the participants to intellectualize over a solution, but it is quite another to put that solution to a demonstrated test. The applied theatre places participants in situations where they are immediately forced to act out possible scenarios.

Given that the participants have developed a commitment to Mel over the episodes through the creation of the artifacts and their hotseating of him, they have an investment in him succeeding. Even if the intervention does not proceed as expected, it is the action that was taken that serves as the catalyst for examination. There is no such thing as failure in the applied theatre. We are working toward improvement—trial and improvement rather than trial and error. The facilitator in the applied theatre is always keen to highlight an aspect of the intervention that was positive.

7. Applied Theatre Is an Aesthetic Medium

The next episode of Mel: *Society at Risk* examines the pressures on those around the protagonist. Previously, we explored different approaches Mel might have pursued in the vignette with his mother and sister. Here, the spotlight is placed on Mel's mother; if time permits, participants could also explore the pressures on Mel's sister Tracey. This strategy is called *autobiographical sketches*.

The actor who played Mel's mother comes forward. The participants are sitting in semicircular rows in front of her. In the following sketch, the group narrates a version of the mother's life that focuses on her past, present, and future. The teaching artist who enacts Mel's mother offers a narrative outline and invites the participants to co-construct the narrative with her. This strategy is somewhat like "fill in the blanks"—the participants are invited to offer their own interpretations of how Mel's mother has controlled/is controlling/will control the circumstances of her life. The emphasis though is on the pressures operating on the mother, how she has managed, what dreams she has for a positive future.

The actor's "sketch" of Mel's mother can include information about her which may have been offered during the hotseating and forum theatre episodes. For instance, if a participant who intervened as Mel during the forum theatre suggested that his mother might not have been a caring and considerate parent, this material could be included in the biographical sketch. The teaching artist needs to draw on the most appropriate material about Mel's mother that has been introduced in the applied theatre project so far.

The teaching artist role-playing Mel's mother begins with a narrative like this:

Actor: I wouldn't say my life has been perfect by any means. Oh, yes, like many others, I've had my ups and downs. Yes, I married when I was quite young, but I did have two beautiful children, Mel and Tracey. Mel, my oldest, worshipped his father. His father had a big impact on him. When Mel was growing up, they both would . . .

The teaching artist fields some suggestions from the participants related to the kind of father–son activities they both would do.

(*continuing*) But, of course, that all changed when he ran off with Jansen. A terrible shock. I had no idea, no forewarning. You see our marriage had been quite happy. We had our arguments, but things were mostly peaceful. Like most families we had a pretty good time and did what might be called normal regular family activities . . .

The teaching artist fields suggestions about the family activities.

The narrative then focuses on:

- Life in the family now
- The changes in Mel's behavior
- Her concerns about Mel
- The pressures on her
- Her dreams about a possible future
- The mother's hopes for her son Mel

At the conclusion of the autobiographical sketch, the facilitator leads a discussion with the participants about the relationship Mel has with his mother.

- *To what extent is this relationship important to Mel?*
- *How might this relationship have an adverse effect on him?*
- *What signs are there that Mel might be personally at risk?*
- *What are the negative forces that might have an impact on him?*

8. Applied Theatre Gives Voice to Communities

In the concluding episode of the applied theatre, participants are provided with opportunities to track circumstances that might lead to a successful transformation of Mel.

Transforming images requires the teaching artist who played Mel to come forward. The facilitator asks the participants to sculpt Mel into a pose that demonstrates how all the negative forces are impacting on him. The facilitator explains that it would be helpful if the group could build on rather than reject the offerings that are made by the participants.

In the first part of this episode, the participants do not physically change the teaching artist's pose; instructions to be "sad" or "depressed" are not requests for physical changes. Here, they provide instructions to the artist to physically move. The instructions must be quite specific and require a movement of some sort; for example, the participants might say:

> *Bow head*
> *Collapse shoulders*
> *Sit down*
> *Fold legs*
> *Fold arms*
> *Raise left forearm*
> *Support left elbow with right palm*
> *Open left palm*
> *Rest forehead in left palm*
> *Open eyes*
> *Have a blank, expressionless stare*

The teaching artist follows the instructions as they are given by the participants. The facilitator has the challenging task of ensuring that all the participants are relatively satisfied with the image as it is being demonstrated in front of them.

The second half of this episode requires all participants to mirror the final image of Mel. Everyone assumes the image of the teaching artist, and the facilitator explains that he or she will count from one to five. With each number, the participants will gradually transform themselves into the counterimage of the negative one being demonstrated. In other words, participants are searching to find a more positive and affirming image of Mel—an image that shows he is now in control of the negative forces and is building a productive future for himself. As the count proceeds—1, 2, 3, 4, 5—a gradual transformation occurs in Mel, from the victim of the negative to a seeker of the positive.

The transforming images are then shared around the participants. The qualities of them are "unpacked." Questions about the various images are asked by the facilitator; examples include:

- *What physical transformations demonstrate a more positive future?*
- *What is different about these second images of Mel?*

IN CONCLUSION

The example program, Mel: *Society at Risk,* concludes with a culminating discussion about the steps or interventions that would need to take place in Mel's life so that those second images can be reached. The facilitator is not aiming to find easy solutions to difficult problems, but rather helps the participants brainstorm some of the intervening steps that need to occur in Mel's life before he is on the road to a positive recovery.

Mel: *Society at Risk,* an applied theatre program, opens up a conversation about at-risk young people and how society might commit to helping them. While Mel is not sitting on the edge of a cliff threatening to jump, or lying on a bathroom floor with a needle in his arm, there are elements in his life that suggest that one of those places is where he could end up. This program begins a process of interrogation. It is not judgmental in that it is dogmatic about what action needs to be pursued. The teaching artists are open to a variety of possibilities and provide many different lenses through which the work can be viewed.

Readers will have noticed that in the applied theatre we are not concerned with locking participants into one role for too long. Too deep of a submersion into one role freezes participants from being open to the variety of different and shifting perspectives available. The challenge is to try to see Mel's life from many positions—his mother's, his sister's, those of others who are trying to give him support. By projecting ourselves into the lives of others, we might get closer to understanding what powers our lives and those who are different from us.

Applied theatre, like other forms of participatory theatre, is a people's theatre. It demands community presence and action, and it especially requires a commitment to helping others help themselves. As Pompeo-Nogueira (2002) says: "[T]heatre is practiced by the people as a way of empowering communities, listening to their concerns, and encouraging them to voice and solve their problems" (202).

In conclusion, let us be reminded of the eight guiding principles that should govern the design and implementation of the applied theatre:

1. Applied theatre is thoroughly researched.
2. Applied theatre seeks incompleteness.
3. Applied theatre demonstrates possible narratives.
4. Applied theatre is task-oriented.
5. Applied theatre poses dilemmas.
6. Applied theatre interrogates futures.
7. Applied theatre is an aesthetic medium.
8. Applied theatre gives voice to communities.

2

IMPLEMENTING APPLIED THEATRE

As we are beginning to notice, applied theatre draws on many of the techniques and strategies familiar to drama educators. For many years, drama education has been committed to raising participants' ownership of the work. This occurs by engaging the participants in the theatre form by finding approaches to release the spectators, or spect-actors in Boal's terms, to become co-conspirators—to believe that they are responsible for shaping the direction and outcomes of the work.

As well, applied theatre is participatory; that is, it is very much driven by the interests and the needs of the community. It shares much with the theatre for development (TfD) movement in that the issues focused on are usually determined by the community. The teaching artists create scenarios based on their research in the community, following extensive discussion with its members. The scenarios are broken down into scenes or episodes that require participation from the audience.

We have seen in the example about Mel that participation occurred through activities such as hotseating, forum theatre, autobiographical sketches, and transforming images. These strategies are meant to open up a conversation—a dialogue between the participants and the applied theatre. While in TfD there can be a top-down message, which can be shaped by political and funding expediencies, applied theatre does not aim to be doctrinaire or condescending. Ahmed (2002) alerts us to some of the traps of the TfD movement: "These plays are in effect a simplified version of pseudo-Marxist 'agit-prop' plays built on conflict between good (the 'downtrodden people') and evil (the 'village elite'), projecting a clear message of what needs to be done" (212).

It is dangerous for applied theatre to emphasize a moral platitude or to insist on a course of action. Simple solutions to life's problems rarely address the complex and challenging dilemmas in which people find themselves.

Even worse, Ahmed argues there is little thorough examination of the issues powering the applied theatre. He believes there is an attitude that the participants are not competent enough to examine the issues presented or, even worse, that the artists are just doing a job. The performers, he cynically ponders, are more interested in "counting their money" than raising "people's critical consciousness concerning social and economic reality" (2002, 212). While wondering who the TfD movement actually serves, Ahmed appeals for a theatre that is always developing—"theatre which allows debate, dialogue, reflexivity, dreaming the impossible and the flight to infinity" (218). These goals are very much shared by the applied theatre.

Our example of *Mel: Society at Risk* has begun to alert us to the purposes of the applied theatre and for whom the work is meant. Clearly, the notion of change is central to the mission of applied theatre, just as it is to the TfD counterpart. This is why the work of Paulo Freire is critical to both movements in that it aims for a kind of liberation theology—to change the circumstances of our lives through a critical active consciousness. Brazilian educator Freire was concerned with enlivening people's capacity to more fully see the world in which they live and to view their own roles and responsibilities in the world more critically. Freire was most interested in the circumstances that powered a *praxis*—the ability to reflect critically on one's actions in order to change the circumstances in which one is living. Change is at the center of praxis.

In this chapter, we continue to examine how applied theatre renders change in the community. We begin by discussing the notion of praxis, and applied theatre praxis in which teaching artists work in collaboration with communities so that they can jointly engage in a dialogue about change and transformation. The challenges in the implementation of an applied theatre are outlined and the compromises these challenges sometimes force are discussed here.

APPLIED THEATRE PRAXIS

Applied theatre praxis refers to the manipulation of theatre form by leaders to help participants act, reflect, and transform. At the core of it is the artful interplay between three elements—people, passion, and platform, the three *ps*—as leaders and participants strive to attain aesthetic understanding.

People

Applied theatre is a collaborative group art form in which people transform, act, and reflect on the human condition. In applied theatre, people are the instruments of inquiry. So far, we have seen how participants in the Mel project entered the dramatic fiction— they stepped into roles, hotseated characters, and transformed their bodies into images of the pressures on the protagonists. The great Russian theatre director Stanislavski ([1949] 1987) argues the importance of this human manipulation. "People," he suggests, "generally do not know how to make use of the physical apparatus with which nature has endowed [them]." The physical self is at the center of a dramatic encounter and applied theatre participants are encouraged as to how best to manipulate their "instrument" (35). Although notions of manipulation seem subversive and harmful, the arts depend on the direct molding, rendering, and manipulating of content into form.

Shakespeare's character, Hamlet, is well aware of the critical role the human instrument plays when assigning meaning. Hamlet's instructions to the players prior to the performance of "The Murder of Gonzago" capture the skills the actors must bring to their parts:

> Speak the speech, I pray you, as I pronounced it to you, trippingly on the tongue; but if you mouth it, as many of your players do, I had as lief the town-crier spoke my lines. Nor do not saw the air too much with your hand, thus; but use all gently: for in the very torrent, tempest, and, as I may say, the whirlwind of your passion, you must acquire and beget a temperance that may give

it smoothness. O it offends me to the soul to hear a robustious periwig-pated fellow tear a passion to tatters. (*Hamlet* III:ii)

Hamlet knows the power of the human instrument and, when artfully put to good use, it can create transformative experiences. Witness a scene from "The Murder of Gonzago"—Hamlet has deliberately selected this play because he believes it mirrors many of the events happening in his own life. He does not have firm evidence to prove that his father was murdered but believes the play will provide the evidence he needs. So, the audience becomes fascinated by the various degrees of watching: the audience watches the play; Hamlet watches Claudius watching "The Murder of Gonzago"; and the other characters watch each other watching Claudius watching. Hamlet does not want the players to ham up their acting; he is on a mission to use the play and the actors' physicalization to "catch the conscience of the King."

Yet, it is not only the physical self that signs meaning—the inner or psychological self needs equally to be understood, to be manipulated if messages are to be successfully conveyed. If you like, participants in applied theatre are split into two parts. Actors live, weep, and laugh on the stage, continues Stanislavski (1949] 1987), but as they do so, they observe and control themselves in the action: "It is this double existence, this balance between life and acting that makes for art" (167).

Art in applied theatre praxis is a conscious manipulation of people in time and space. This, then, leads to the second key element—passion.

Passion

I am using the term *passion* to refer to a heightened state, which can arouse strong and emotive responses. In applied theatre, *passion* refers to the fictitious world where the participants find themselves, a world that demands people to momentarily step into imagined roles, characters, and situations. Shakespeare referred to his theatre as "a fiction . . . a dream of passion" (1957, II:ii). In the Christian liturgical year, *the passion* refers to the narrative of Christ's crucifixion. The passion, then, is the unfolding tale, the stories that contain, as Hamlet says, the "abstracts and brief chronicles of the time" (Shakespeare 1957, II:ii) in which we live.

In his book *The Rainbow of Desire*, South American theatre director Augusto Boal (1995) argues that theatre cannot exist without passion. He likens theatre to a passionate combat of two human beings on a platform. "Theatre denotes conflict, contradiction, confrontation and defiance," he argues, quoting the work of the Spanish dramatist Lope de Vega (16). Theatre is a passion, a heightened state, which elevates and focuses attention to another plane.

For my purposes, I will broaden this definition to encompass the created world that people conspire to make, present, and reflect on. While that passion might involve "combat," it does not always. I am attracted to the argument of British educator Gavin Bolton, who was one of the first leaders to acknowledge how clumsy the term *conflict* can be when describing theatre activity. For Bolton (1979), drama expresses the constraints on the expression of a conflict. If we look at the features of theatre form, we note how often characters find themselves in situations where they are prevented from expressing who they are.

In Shakespeare's play, Hamlet is prevented from expressing his view that Claudius killed his father because he feels he needs more evidence and solicits the players' help in this endeavor. George and Martha, throughout the play *Who's Afraid of Virginia Woolf* (Albee 1965), are not able to accept how they have created a fictitious child to stop them from confronting the kind of shallow lives they have constructed for themselves. The male characters in *The Weir* (McPherson 1999), simultaneously, are not in conflict with one another in the play but rather are constrained by their life circumstances to express the kind of human beings they are and those they aspire to become. We can all think of other examples of where the heart of the theatre is located in the situations that prevent truths from being revealed.

Often in applied theatre, it is when the conflict between, or within, the characters is expressed that the curtain comes down and the play ends. The drama does not focus on the conflict between characters, but on the forces operating on characters that inhibit or constrain the expression of conflict. In the Mel project, the task for the teaching artists was not to solve the puzzle of Mel but to keep the options open. The trick is to try to have as many different readings of Mel as possible during the early stages of the work so that participants can each create their own understanding of him. Participants in applied theatre are more likely to commit to situations when they feel they have some control over shaping and directing them.

The Platform

I am not referring here to a raised area where the passion is performed, although applied theatre does occur on elevated physical platforms. I am referring to that marked space, what Boal describes as the aesthetic space, where people creating passions live. Such platforms, aesthetic spaces, can be in classrooms, on streets, in hospitals, at business organizations. The TfD movement, for example, works in a variety of village and community locales that are shared by applied theatre artists.

Throughout time, these locales have been marked in a variety of ways—around campfires, on horse-drawn carriages, in fields. We know that in Elizabethan times actors were pretty much strolling players performing plays wherever they found a friendly audience. Sometimes, they would create platform spaces on the back of their carts although a much yearned-for setting would be an inn yard where proximity between actors and spectators was intimate; as Day (1996) argues, this is a setting that later was "deliberately copied in the eventual design of the amphitheatres" (6).

The formality of mainstream theatre houses is but one space in which passions can occur, perhaps the more conventional space, certainly from the time of Shakespeare. But the praxis of applied theatre pushes the boundaries of those mainstream houses into a variety of vocational, community, and educational settings—parks, street fares, hospital wards, business training sites, police stations, conference venues.

The notion of the *applied* theatre is that theatre is pressed onto something other than itself. Like applied mathematics, applied psychology, applied chemistry, it is the concrete rather than the abstract that is being reinforced (i.e., that which can be used and seen). Applying theatre to teach literacy, applying theatre to interrogate domestic violence, applying theatre to understand oppression—each of these recognizes the power of the theatre form as a powerful educative medium.

What is common to the platform spaces, wherever they be, is that people and passions occur on them and that audiences engage with them. In the applied theatre though, the audience is the participants themselves as they work toward aesthetic understanding.

Aesthetic Understanding

Aesthetic, a word that has confounded and perplexed commentators for some time, refers to how satisfying we find the artwork and how well it massages our senses. My colleague Maxine Greene, the eminent American philosopher, argues that aesthetic education requires people to attend to artworks with discrimination and authenticity. By that she refers to a capacity for people to understand how the form manipulates the content, and vice versa.

In applied theatre praxis, then, we want participants to be able to manipulate the elements of their craft (people, passion, and platforms) and to understand how that manipulation works so that audiences can appreciate and be transformed through the medium. It takes a lot of understanding, argues Greene, to understand how art conspires to generate meaning.

And, the purposes of aesthetic understanding are? Yes, there are the functional and communication skills, which can be developed, and the social habits, which can be refined, but these skills are not dependent on applied theatre praxis; there are other curriculum areas that deal with them. The reasons for applied theatre praxis are the insights to be made, the revelations to be had. "The play's the thing/Wherein I'll catch the conscience of the King" (Shakespeare 1957, II:ii), states Hamlet, fully aware of the power of the art form to raise levels of consciousness. The arts' role through the generations has been to "chronicle the time," to unfold the nature of our lives and the world in which we live. If operated well, applied theatre is a powerful educative medium.

Praxis

For many years now, the word *practice* has suggested something quite different from theory. Practice connoted the doing, the active, the process. *Theory* connoted the not-doing, the thinking about, the product. Unfortunately, such words—theory, practice—led to unhealthy divisions between those who thought or wrote about theatre compared with those who did and practiced theatre.

The thinkers couldn't practice, and the practitioners weren't thinkers, or so the argument went. The word *praxis*, though, brings these two aspects of theory and practice together, seeing both as a part of a complex dynamic encounter.

We who have a commitment to applied theatre are aware that many of the great practitioners are equally the great theorists. Augusto Boal (2001), an amazing practitioner, provided a secure theoretical framework on which many of the principles of applied theatre are soundly based. Dorothy Heathcote (Bolton 2003), perhaps the most talented educational drama practitioner of the twentieth century, who provided a conceptual understanding of what drama was for and how to implement it, has transformed generations of educators. While working predominantly within drama classrooms in British schools, many of the techniques she developed, such as teacher in role and image theatre, can be readily adapted to an applied theatre setting. Both Boal and Heathcote cannot simply be labeled as practitioners or theoreticians, but bring together a blend of theory and practice that informs it.

I much prefer the term *applied theatre praxis* to *applied theatre practice*. *Praxis*, a word developed by Brazilian educator Paulo Freire (1970), claims that an ability to help one another reflect and act on their world is at the heart of a sound education, and through that process transforms it into something more equitable and worthwhile. Praxis is powered by an agenda, a desire to push us to reflect on our practices and refine our theoretical leanings as a step toward acting on and changing our life circumstances. Put simply, praxis denotes the action, reflection, and transformation of people as they engage with one another. Those involved in praxis can anticipate that such action, reflection, and transformation should help people create a just and better world. And, this is where applied theatre can play a major role.

Let's now look at three different applied theatre projects, how they were implemented, and the challenges they raise for the field.

THREE PROJECTS

People, passion, and the platform—the three *ps*—are central to applied theatre. In this section, I deconstruct the characteristics of another three *ps*—three *projects* focused on vandalism, on racism, and on teenage pregnancy. They were commissioned by government agencies interested in raising community consciousness. In each, we shall observe how the careful manipulation of people, passion, and platform was central to the projects' successful implementation.

The agencies were particularly interested in the work of the South American theatre director Augusto Boal (see Boal 1995), and asked whether the programs could be devised to include audience participation techniques to problem solve issues faced by the community. As we know, Boal is renowned for developing the forum theatre technique, or the people's theatre. Using this format, audience members participate directly in interrogating an issue presented to them by actors. The audience is familiar with the issue and is interested in resolving it in a positive, constructive manner. Boal's forum theatre has been particularly successful in facilitating conversation and action with marginalized groups, so it and other participatory strategies lend themselves ideally to the applied theatre.

The agencies were determined that the work place the problem-solving responsibility on the audience (hereafter referred to as *participants*) for the situations being presented by the actors. Because they had no experience with commissioning applied theatre, the agencies were concerned that the issues would not be too controversial.

I am going to refer to the general qualities that powered the implementation of these projects rather than to provide specific descriptions of the projects themselves. These descriptions have been written about elsewhere and do not bear repeating here (see Taylor 2002a, 2002b). My concern is to highlight the teaching and design principles that informed the projects' evolution and to examine the challenges these pose for applied theatre workers. I am hopeful that readers will be able to isolate the principles and use them in the construction of their own applied theatre work.

Common to applied theatre projects is a commitment to community change. Applied theatre operates from a realization that there are issues within communities that need addressing and that participatory theatre is one way of dealing with them. For example, applied theatre might help communities address topics related to too much vandalism to public property, alarming increases in racist slurs, and an increase in teenage pregnancies. In the communities where the following projects took place, these issues were of concern.

Although attempts had been made to combat the problems with public service notices and various media campaigns, there seemed to have been little change in the incidence of vandalism, racism, and teenage pregnancy. Thus, community members decided on the applied theatre approach to address the issues. The applied theatre program would aim to:

- Raise the community's level of consciousness so that residents can begin to freely and openly discuss the issues
- Generate dialogue for individuals in the community to help them reach personal and collective goals

Government agencies, of course, have an interest in curbing the amount of monies that go into social services programs. From the agencies' point of view, if the theatre groups could help change community consciousness then their financial investment in the theatre work would be money well spent. This immediately places applied theatre artists in an unenviable position in that they now share the responsibility to curb vandalism, racism, and teenage pregnancy. Applied theatre artists need to be careful that they don't merely become mouthpieces for a government or bureaucratic agenda. The aim of the applied theatre artist should be to open up a conversation around a particular issue and challenge community members to use this theatre form as a way to further that conversation.

Within this context, agencies that commission such work can be quick to blame the residents for the problems in their communities. I recall working on one project for which I was provided with a government newsletter that dealt with the problem of community apathy.[1] The funding agent referred to the high levels of

---

[1]New South Wales (Australia), *Department of Housing Community Renewal Strategy Newsletter* 1(1) (brochure). Brisbane: Author.

apathy and highlighted the reluctance of community members to become actively involved in their own affairs:

What Makes Life Dreary Is Want of Motive
   Apathy is the state of those people who don't want to get involved in what you are offering. Are they apathetic—or perhaps just not interested in the same issues you are? People have a right to decide their own interests and purpose, and their own level of participation. There is a fine line between creating awareness and telling people what they should have or do. What appears to be apathy may also be anxiety about becoming involved in something new and uncertain.

Although this statement highlights the complex nature of the lack of involvement, it also places the onus on the community to become more involved in local issues. If change doesn't happen, the argument suggests, it could very well be because of community residents' apathetic responses rather than the inability of the government agency to effect change. There seemed to be an implication that apathy was a problem that the residents had; in other words, residents' apathy did not promote change, which was a continual source of irritation to the government agencies.

So when applied theatre work is commissioned, the artists might find themselves caught within a range of agendas focused on the commissioning agents' needs and demands, and the realities of what is or is not possible within a short space of time. We must remember that applied theatre is but one tool of the community worker to effect change; by no means is it the only tool.

The projects in the sections that follow had an expectation that the applied theatre work would facilitate group consciousness and place participants in situations where they could resolve many of the issues causing them, and the agency, discomfort. As well, there was interest in community renewal whereby notions of full participation and change would be emphasized, enabling people to activate their consciousness to help people see their own realities and how they might transform those realities that impact them negatively.

Notions of participation—inclusivity and enabling of people to take control over their lives—are central principles of applied theatre. In each of the following descriptions, a site visit to the area precipitated development of the applied theatre. At these site visits, observations were made on general happenings within the community. Using the techniques of the fieldworker, or those engaged by qualitative researchers, logbooks were kept to document the teaching artists' observations during the visit. Interviews with residents were conducted, conversations about how applied theatre might be relevant to residents' needs took place, and pamphlets outlining the history of the site were collected at the same time general demographic material was being gathered.

The site visit emphasized the importance of the notion of a partnership between teaching artist and community. The teaching artists told everyone they were not entering the communities as experts or authorities who had a message, but rather as collaborators who would work together with the stakeholders. Each of the projects occurred in rural sites where unemployment was high, especially among young people. Most of the sites were isolated from large cities so there was no access to the resources and facilities that can be found in densely packed urban communities.

◆ A PROJECT ON TEENAGER VANDALISM OF PROPERTY

The visit to the site where this project was to be presented demonstrated that youth felt alienated from their seniors, vandalism provided something for kids to do, and absconding from police by jumping fences was a popular activity. The division between adults and kids appeared a prevalent theme, and historical and inherent racism was evident. The white and indigenous children did not seem to mix; white kids didn't seem to understand black kids. There appeared to be tension between the government departments and the residents. Racist attitudes seemed to stem from a belief that unemployment was high in the minority groups. There were problems of alcohol abuse, especially with young kids, and a sense of futility and resignation to the deprived circumstances of one's life. Finally, local government departments didn't understand what the Residents Associations was.

This applied theatre project was to be presented in outdoor venues—parks, street fares, and shopping malls. The intention was to have a wide-ranging audience who could jointly interrogate the issues Rachel, the protagonist, is experiencing. The aim was not to be too heavy-handed about public property vandalism—sometimes a response to authority or a desire to not follow societal conventions—because, if applied theatre becomes too didactic, participants feel they are being preached at. Were the program too doctrinaire, it would have had little or no impact.

Into this context, a group of applied theatre artists come with the intention of generating dialogue about teenage vandalism through the eyes of Rachel.

Guiding Questions

- *Why do teenagers vandalize public property?*
- *What advice might the participants give a teenager who enjoys vandalism and who has a track record of such offenses with the police?*

Scenario

The program focuses on a seventeen-year-old girl, Rachel, caught vandalizing public property and arrested by the police. While at the police station, she is questioned about her regular defacement of public property. She responds by saying that she is "bored" and that spraying paint on fences is "something to do." Rachel is cocky and says there is nothing wrong with painting fences—the township needs a "facelift" anyway.

When the police leave her for a moment, Rachel dreams of a better life. She has lived on the housing (residential) estate since she was born. Her dad left when she was twelve, and she hasn't spoken to him or seen him in five years. She wants to go to live with her boyfriend Jack, but he seems uncommitted to her and is more concerned with his own interests. While dreaming of a better life with Jack, Rachel sees an opportunity to escape from the police station. She does so. This concludes the performance presentation.

Participatory Work

The program presents scenes from Rachel's life. The participants witness some of the problems she is experiencing in her home life—not being able to communicate with her mother, dealing with an absent father. Her relationship with her boyfriend, Jack, is outlined; Rachel dreams of going to live with Jack. The participants are asked to brainstorm Rachel's alternatives.

- How might she productively deal with her situation?
- If she decided to leave home, where might she go?

The participants become Rachel's conscience and voice some thoughts that might go through her mind. They stand in a circle and the teaching artist playing Rachel comes around to each of the participants and voices her conscience. This is known as *conscience-alley*, sometimes referred to as thought-tracking, which enables participants to voice the private feelings and desires of characters.[2] Often, participants project their own desires into the thought processes of the protagonist.

The participants hotseat Rachel; they directly experience her anger toward her elders, her dislike of school, her hatred of herself. She explains why she likes vandalizing public property. Volunteers from the participant audience represent the fence that Rachel has symbolically constructed around herself. They now are the barriers that Rachel endures.

The facilitator asks: What are the barriers she faces? How will she overcome these barriers? How will she break down the fences? In an ideal world, Rachel will be able to break through the barriers. The teaching artist playing Rachel mimes breaking through the fence by gently pushing participants aside.

The program concludes with a facilitator asking participants to consider whether Rachel's character is familiar to them. Have they come across a Rachel before? What can society do to help the Rachels of this world? What can they as individuals do to help Rachel?

Comments

This program requires three teaching artists: the facilitator, Rachel, the multi-role—police, mother, Jack. The facilitator can assume a role in the applied theatre if needed.

The situation of Rachel must hold strong resonance for the participants if it is to hold their interest. The challenge of working in large open spaces requires teaching artists who can draw the participants into the work. This may require them to encourage

---

[2]For a list of excellent conventions that applied theatre artists can draw on, see Neelands and Goode (2000).

participants to move up closer to the platform. The intention is to eventually get participants on the platform, where they can begin to directly demonstrate how they might go about helping someone like Rachel. Remember, I am using the word *platform* here as the marked space, the aesthetic space, where the applied theatre world operates; I am not referring to a raised stage as one might find in a conventional theatre. Again, the teaching artists are not the ones solving the puzzle. The onus is on participants to enter a dialogue about their commitment to helping Rachel.

If the audience detects that too strong a message is being played out, or that the applied theatre is simply an instrument of the state (i.e., to bring the audience into line about the criminality of vandalism), they will lose interest and could intentionally try to disturb the project. A strength of this program is that it considers the options for someone in Rachel's situation and demonstrates that she is not alone in her thoughts.

Interestingly enough, at one of the project's performances, a government agency representative who attended was not satisfied that our presentation had made its point. For instance, concern was expressed by the agent that there was no statement about the ills of vandalism when Rachel was spraying paint on a fence. The teaching artists did not lecture participants about defacement of property. Clearly, the commissioning agency was hoping the program would be more assertive about correct behavior.

In my experience, however, when applied theatre is too insistent on the proper course of action, the aesthetic moment is weakened, preventing genuine dialogue and conversation about the issue being addressed. Besides, in the program we had devised, Rachel was arrested by the police because of her actions. What greater penalty could be had?

◆ A PROJECT ABOUT RACISM IN A SMALL TOWN

The visit to the site demonstrated that this project's location had a high population of indigenous people. The youth of the township had low self-esteem and were doing poorly at school. Nevertheless, there was a powerful sense of community and the notion of an extended family present.

The commissioning agency informed me that the theatre work would take place at a community center for the indigenous youth located on the housing project where many of them lived. This project was annexed from the main town that was two or three miles away. The center had a medical and counseling facility where young people and their families could receive free advice on a range of issues. Also, important was the fact that the center was a drop-in location for youth; they could just hangout there. During the site visit, we noticed that kids of all ages would wander in and out of the center, just checking on each other, seeing what was happening.

The site visit suggested that the township's youth were experiencing violence, drugs, poverty, racism, and anger. I had been requested to create a program to help young people who drop in at the community center build self-esteem and a better group image and to think positively about how they might respond to any racial slurs they experience. The program was to be presented at the center on a Saturday morning for twenty or more young people of ages varying from eight to twenty.

Guiding Questions
- *How can applied theatre help build a sense of self and community identity?*
- *How should victims of racial slurs respond to aggressors?*

Scenario
The applied theatre program focuses on identity or, more important, the lack of identity. The facilitator leads the group through some icebreakers to focus attention and maintain interest. Circle Dash is played. Here the group stands in a circle with one person in the middle. The aim of the activity is for the person in the middle to get to the circle's perimeter. This can happen only when two people standing in the circle make eye contact, then exchange places. While the exchange is happening, the middle person, noticing that a place on the circle's perimeter has opened up, attempts to take it. The activity continues as the person who is not able to trade places successfully goes to the middle.[3]

---

[3]For further examples of ice-breaking activities, see Rodd (1998).

The facilitator asks the group what skills are required to play this activity successfully. The group then meets someone who had great trouble playing these activities and others like them at school.

The facilitator introduces the group to twenty-two-year-old Sarah. A teaching artist enters as Sarah. The facilitator explains that Sarah had difficulty concentrating at school and often failed to remember the rules of most activities, like Circle Dash. She was clumsy and was made fun of a lot by her fellow students.

Sarah explains that she hates playing games like Circle Dash at school. While everyone else enjoys them, she doesn't. Sarah tells the story of her life, how she dislikes school and always feels that she grew up on "the wrong side of the tracks." The teaching artist Sarah tells of her experience trying to survive in her small town, highlighting the underage drinking, the binge drinking, the rave parties, the pill popping. Sarah says she hates living in such a small town where everybody seems to know everybody else's business.

Sarah tells them of a recurring dream that she has of being tied to railway tracks as a train approaches. In the dream, people are standing around her laughing, calling her names, making racial slurs, telling her she has no future. Sarah ends her monologue with, "I am proud to be a black woman."

Participatory Work

The facilitator asks what kind of life Sarah must be leading. They describe her life as it might have been for her while growing up. Participants discuss the kind of influences on her. The facilitator asks what she meant by, "I am proud to be a black woman."

The participants are encouraged to talk about Sarah's dream. They are enrolled as expert dream therapists who must "decode" what the dream means. Volunteers are asked to come forward. One plays Sarah tied to the tracks; two or three others stand behind her making train engine sounds. Two or three others stand to the side of Sarah and yell out abusive names and slurs—the kinds of things that might have been said to Sarah in her dream. The facilitator aims to create a nonlinear text that emphasizes moments rather than well-rounded narratives. The action is frozen and mimed. The sounds are drawn out, and movements are exaggerated. This scene will need to be replayed by the facilitator so that the volunteers are comfortable with the text they have created. It does not need to run longer than thirty seconds. Participants discuss the elements of the dream. What questions does this dream pose for us about Sarah? The participants, in role as therapists, brainstorm what the dream means for Sarah:

- What does being tied to the tracks suggest?
- What might the train represent?
- Who is Sarah frightened of?
- What might happen to Sarah if these dreams continue?

The participants then meet Sarah, the original teaching artist, again. The facilitator explains that things have deteriorated for her. Her dreams have become more frequent and she has not spoken in some time. The participants try to speak to her as therapists but to no avail. Sarah repeats, "I am proud to be a black woman." Participants then create scenes from Sarah's life to try to suggest why she might be having the dream and why she constantly says the same thing.

The facilitator explains that contained within the scene is an oppressor—someone who is restricting Sarah from being who she wants to be. What might have happened to Sarah that led her to constantly repeat the phrase, "I am proud to be a black woman"? The participants work on the scenes, and one is selected and workshopped as a forum theatre. The participants try to problem solve, looking for alternatives to the oppression Sarah is experiencing in the scene.

Comments

This program will work with two teaching artists—one who plays the facilitating role and one who is Sarah. Because the applied theatre was to be presented in a community center where acoustics were not a problem and where it was easy to focus attention, emphasis was placed on having participants generate scenes from Sarah's past that led to her feeling alienated. While these scenes might focus on racist incidents, they didn't need to. Sarah's words—"I am proud to be a black woman"—must have inspired the scene.

Emphasis is placed on constructing forum theatre scenes; the group needs to ensure that the actor playing Sarah is clearly in a failing position. For instance, the Sarah character might be the victim of racial taunts at school, taunts she cannot stop. Alternatively, at one of the parties Sarah attends, pressure might be placed on her to have sex, a pressure that she finds she cannot resist. As the scene is rehearsed, the facilitator reminds the group to make the source of Sarah's oppression clear: Who is responsible for victimizing Sarah in the scenes? How does this victimization occur? Why is Sarah incapable of overcoming victimization?

After the scenes have been shared, the facilitator explains that they will pick a scene that clearly presents Sarah's dilemma to do a forum theatre. It needs to reinforce that she is failing to overcome her oppression. The scene is replayed and the audience is invited to *stop* the action at a specific moment when Sarah could have done something different—an action, a statement, a gesture—to change her oppression. Remind participants to call out "stop" at just that moment.

When alternatives are suggested, the participants come forward to act out their solutions by taking Sarah's place. The emphasis is on resolving the situation from within the art form rather than discussing what action might have taken place. Following various attempts to rebuild Sarah, the group has a conversation about how effective the strategy was.

It is important for the facilitator to emphasize the positive actions of the Sarahs in transforming her plight from a state of victimhood to a state of being in control. Any portrayal of an action that builds a positive future should be welcomed by the facilitator. The group needs to believe that Sarah does have more productive options. The participatory activities must enable the group to create a useful dialogue around the issues faced by the protagonist Sarah. Forum theatre work should provoke much interest on the part of participants because they have created their own scenes as spontaneous proposed solutions to transform oppressive states. Audience participation is critical to the success of this program.

◆ A PROGRAM ON TEENAGE PREGNANCY

A site visit to a rural township revealed that teenage pregnancy was a huge problem. While there was knowledge about safe-sex practices, there seemed to be little interest in contraception. The principal industry in this town was livestock, raising cattle. Indeed, wherever one looked, there were pictures of cows. The residents seemed to pride themselves on the town's reputation as being a beef capital.

Interviews with the young people reinforced a sense of isolation and boredom. There seemed to be little for the youth to do in this township; for instance, there were no game parlors, no community centers where they could meet. The local convenience store seemed to be the only place to congregate after school and on weekends.

The lack of recreational facilities meant that many traveled to a city ten miles away to engage in pleasurable leisure activities. The commissioning agency requested that we design a project to deal with teenage pregnancy to be presented to community members in a center at one of the housing projects. We were to work with high school students in the creation of the project and include opportunities for the wider community to become involved in the presentation. It was clear from our interviews with the young people that they believed the adults of the town had little interest in them. Because the program was to include local high school students, it was important that their voices should inform the direction of the theatre work. The students were happy that this work was to focus on teenage pregnancy, but they saw this issue as a community problem, not simply a problem of young people. Students were glad that the program was going to demand participation from the adult community; they expected the elders to accept responsibility and to help young people find solutions to community problems.

Guiding Questions
- *How can theatre form be used to explore teenage pregnancy?*
- *How might community elders accept responsibility for teenage pregnancy?*

Scenario

Three teaching artists work with the high school students for two days to create a program focusing on teenage pregnancy. The teaching artists explain that this work must deal with teenage pregnancy but that the actual details of the program are to be negotiated by the whole group.

They begin by creating a role by drawing the outline of a human body on paper on the wall. The group is told that this outline represents a pregnant teenager. On the inside of the outline, participants write or draw what this girl's dreams are. What does she want in her life? What are her goals? Where might she hope to be in ten years? What are her favorite shows? Books? Songs?

The space outside of the figure is to represent those constraints placed on her: What is preventing her from achieving her dreams? What are the real-life forces this character has to endure? What are her least favorite activities? The participants give this character a name and begin to process more about her life. They begin to construct a portrait of her—let's call her Susan—through a character-building game called *role circle*; each person offers something about the character's life. The facilitator asks the group, in role as Susan, questions like the following:

- *How old are you?*
- *Do you have any brothers and sisters?*
- *How long have you lived here?*
- *Do you like living here, why and/or why not?*
- *Do you go to school?*
- *Do you like school, why and/or why not?*
- *Why do you no longer go to school? Are you happy with this decision, why or why not?*
- *What do you like to do in your spare time?*
- *How do you vent your anger and frustration?*
- *When did you find out that you were pregnant?*
- *How does this news affect you?*

Each participant's response needs to be accepted and built on. The group reconstructs aspects of Susan's daily routine by using the *Hours of the Day* activity. Here, the facilitator calls out times of the day, and the group enacts what Susan might be doing at these times. Participants are then divided into two groups—one presents the Hours of the Day, the other observes.

An image theatre activity follows: the group stands in a circle and recreates how Susan responded when she heard the news that she was pregnant. As the facilitator counts down from five to one, participants slowly sculpt themselves into their representations of Susan when she finds out she's pregnant. Similar images are grouped and then reflected on by the whole group. An image that holds particular resonance for the whole group is selected and becomes the basis for scene work.

The group devises a series of scenes in which Susan experiences a variety of oppressions: from her friends, her boyfriend, the police, her mother. These scenes are then presented to an adult audience who selects one oppression that seems most dominant in Susan's life. The scene the adult audience selects is the one that will be workshopped with the larger group. Time permitting, more than one scene can be workshopped.

Participatory Work

In one scene, the girl's boyfriend decides to move to the city to find work; Susan is dissatisfied with his decision because she is pregnant and needs her boyfriend close by. The boyfriend explains that he is leaving to find work in the interest of the family; however, Susan doesn't know whether to believe him or not. The adult participants hotseat the boyfriend and interrogate him about his motives. An alter-ego strategy is introduced whereby an adult participant is invited to represent the boyfriend's inner thoughts. Standing behind the boyfriend, the adult participant voices his inner thoughts as the boyfriend responds to questions from the audience. The scene with the boyfriend is replayed with the adult participant representing the inner world of the boyfriend; there is a dialogue in the group as to how richly resonant the inner world appears.

In another scene, the girl's mother expresses her dismay about the pregnancy and implies she will have little to do with her daughter. She tries to arrange an abortion, much to Susan's dismay. The adult audience hotseats the mother with the daughter. The adult participants attempt to find a way of reconciling them, but the mother does not seem interested in the adults' advice. Susan's mother believes her daughter has brought disgrace to the family. An alter-ego activity is played out wherein adult participants attempt to get into the inner world of the mother and the daughter. Discussion occurs as to whether this representation is resonant with the experience of parents and children in the community.

Comments

This program was devised by three teaching artists working in partnership with a group of high school students. It was conducted at a community center in a housing project within walking distance to the students' school. A key factor in the successful construction of this work is for the students' voices to inform its execution. The creation of Susan is their own, and ideally, she represents issues they are experiencing.

In this program, we see an emphasis on the devising phase of the applied theatre. Here, the teaching artists work in partnership with the young people to present a participatory program for an adult audience. Applied theatre works wonderfully when there is a genuine sense of collaboration between the stakeholders. This kind of collaboration provokes group ownership. Having the adult audience process the dilemmas young people find themselves in helps present the issue as one of community concern rather than a problem belonging to only one section of the population.

The alter-ego activity is a powerful way of highlighting the tensions between the public face and the private agenda. As the mother and daughter interact with each other, their internal private thoughts are aired. A subtext, which gets at the pressures on community members, is introduced. As adults role-play teenagers in crisis, and as teenagers role-play adults burdened by responsibility and community pressure, a wider conversation emerges about citizenship and survival.

Even though the problems of the world may not be solved, a fruitful dialogue emerges about the quality of our interactions with one another and the extent to which we can understand and share the perspectives of others. Applied theatre uniquely places participants on the inside of an experience where, for a moment in time, they can confront the positions and agendas of a range of perspectives, perhaps different from their own.

IN CLOSING

We are beginning to observe how the applied theatre can be an important "tool kit" for communities to explore what they are and are not capable of achieving. Increasingly, we are seeing a number of governmental and administrative agencies embracing the power

of applied theatre as a way for communities to work more harmo-
niously together, to interrogate the issues of pressing concern to
them, and to jointly consider ways communities can have their
critical consciousness raised.

The three projects described in this chapter were designed by
teaching artists in partnership with the communities who were to
experience the participatory work. It is clear that site visits prior
to implementation of the applied theatre is critical to its successful genesis; site visits facilitate teaching artists' understanding of
what issues are powering the community. When projects have been
commissioned by external agents, site observations can be useful
for corroborating the extent to which the issue being addressed
holds currency within the community. It is critical that the teaching artist be open to the wide range of issues sometimes presented
by the site visits.

Teaching artists are often guests of the community, so they may
not have direct experience about the issue under investigation. It
is critical for the teaching artist to be open-minded and released
from a particular agenda to shape a project in a given prepro-
grammed way. The work documented in this chapter evolves in
action. The outcomes are not determined in advance other than
the constraint of the project dealing with a particular issue, theme,
or question. It is problematic for teaching artists to predict how
participants are going to respond at any given moment. Applied
theatre must include a range of strategies and techniques to facilitate dialogue and to enable participants to voice their own
perspectives. It is these perspectives that are to be subjected to
interrogation.

Teaching artists must be able to read the context in a way that
enables participants to feel valued. Initial aims and objectives
might need to be transformed during the participatory stages. This
then requires a particular skill of teaching artists—adaptation, the
ability to negotiate aims and outcomes in process. The days of
teaching artists following a set packaged program are long gone;
emerging research suggests that the success of arts programs is
largely dependent on teaching artists being able to work in partnership with the principal stakeholders.

Applied theatre is powered by community needs and should be
a bottom-up process driven by grassroots concerns. Although this

might place teaching artists in a difficult position in terms of meeting the needs of funding organizations while collaborating in the field, community change is only going to occur when there is a demonstrated commitment to honoring the views and input of all of its members. The qualities of an effective partnership in applied theatre are the focus of the next chapter.

3

THE APPLIED THEATRE
TEACHING ARTIST

In the previous chapter, I argued how the elements of applied theatre involved an artistic manipulation of three elements—people, passion, and the platform. In effect, these three elements are partnered together as teaching artists generate powerful aesthetic experiences. However, we could also say that a wider partnership is necessary if applied theatre praxis is to be managed well; it should be a partnership not only between the three elements but between the teaching artists, the participants, the community, and all the various stakeholders who are invested in the success of applied theatre. Clearly, it is useful to consider the work of applied theatre as a partnership.

This chapter examines the skills teaching artists need to develop in order to create satisfying partnerships with the various stakeholders. The term *teaching artists* refers to the actors who tour with applied theatre programs. In some ways, they are like the traditional theatre troupe, the strolling players if you will, who take their theatre programs into a range of different settings and sites. There is one significant difference, however; they are named teaching artists because they must bring both the skills of presenting theatre work and the rare ability to act as educators who can help process the program's teaching points with diverse groups. Sometimes the term *actor–teacher* is used interchangeably with *teaching artists*. I prefer the term *teaching artist* in the applied theatre because it highlights the pedagogical function, which should drive the leaders' artistry.

In the applied theatre, the artists' teaching skills are just as important, if not more so, than theatrical presentation for it is in the teaching ability of the artists that the *applied* nature of the work will be realized. In other words, that part of the work that can help us learn something we didn't know before, challenge entrenched ideas, or even examine corrupt and damaging views of the world. Applied theatre can support community action by bringing forward what was previously felt but unsaid and can now be aired and examined.

Teaching artists need to be able to draw participants into the imaginary world; they must be able to find the appropriate stance, gesture, question, or attitude that will enable the participants to notice what needs to be noticed. The teaching artist should have the skills to assist participants to dialogue with each other and with the other teaching artists. Teaching artists need to put participants' anxieties to rest so that they can practically and willingly engage with the work and reflect on its pertinent features.

Teaching artists need to be good conversationalists, but they should also be able to read constructed text and monitor how participants are responding to the presentation and to the activities at any given point. Effective teaching artists are effective educators who are capable of inspiring enthusiasm and commitment to focused subject matter. The best material is most effectively realized when teaching artists have the ability to engage and to empower participants to take ownership of the material. When participants feel they own the material, they are more likely to embrace it as significant to them.

This chapter describes how teaching artists can garner the skills required to make applied theatre happen. Because little has been written about the qualities good teaching artists need, I will draw on inspiring illustrations of good drama praxis from the field of drama in education and relate them to applied theatre teaching artists' work.

The central principles of applied theatre praxis as outlined in Chapter 1 are discussed here in relation to the challenges they raise for teaching artists. I will demonstrate how successful teaching artists in applied theatre praxis need to

- *Activate* themselves in order to perform a dual role—artist–educator

- *Reflect* on their contributions to the applied theatre partnership
- *Transform* understandings of the participants' worldview

These are the three qualities—action, reflection, transformation (ART)—of the applied theatre.

Applied theatre partnerships provide experiences that change and transform us, experiences that provoke good and sometimes unsettling questions, and experiences that both please and educate. One key condition for a successful partnership is the power of the artwork created; the discussion here focuses on how the artwork, the artistic products, and the scenarios can empower the presentation and engage participants so that a successful partnership emerges.

A SATISFYING APPLIED THEATRE

Remember, the first chapter outlined what the key characteristics or principles for creating applied theatre should be. These principles contain particular challenges for the teaching artists; it is those challenges that are highlighted next.

Eight Principles for Planning Applied Theatre

1. *Applied theatre is thoroughly researched*—Teaching artists need to fully comprehend what issues are involved in creating the applied theatre. Why is applied theatre a powerful way to address a particular issue? Visits to the communities where the project will be implemented are necessary in advance of the design phase. Interviewing a range of community members is necessary so that teaching artists can create appropriate scenarios that resonant with the experiences of the community. Participants need to feel that they *own* the applied theatre project from the outset.

2. *Applied theatre seeks incompleteness*—Teaching artists must be careful that the programs created do not pose simple solutions to life's problems; there need to be opportunities for participants to negotiate the content and the direction of the work. There should be significant gaps in the program so that participants can present

their own versions of reality and their own understanding of the interventions that might be applicable at any given moment.

3. *Applied theatre demonstrates possible narratives*—Teaching artists need to present a range of options from which decisions about necessary choices can be made. These options might be equally compelling and might place participants in uncomfortable intellectual positions when decisions are selected. Participants must be able to provide their own version, or narrative, of events, especially when there is some disagreement about the choices and the motivations evident in the work.

4. *Applied theatre is task-oriented*—Teaching artists need to establish activities in which participants can begin to directly enter the protagonist's experience. Concrete tasks need to be offered so that participants can momentarily step into another's perspective or confront the situation the protagonist has encountered. From this experience of participating within the fictional event, participants can embrace firsthand the issues on which the applied theatre focuses.

5. *Applied theatre poses dilemmas*—Teaching artists understand that at the heart of applied theatre is the recognition that choices are central to human behavior. Protagonists are either successful or unsuccessful based on the determinations they make about actions. Such choices can be difficult, especially when consequences are involved. Often, the alternatives before a protagonist can be jointly compelling or contradictory, ambiguous, and unclear. Teaching artists help participants tolerate ambiguity and the struggle with contradictions.

6. *Applied theatre interrogates futures*—Teaching artists are able to raise good questions rather than answer simple ones. Applied theatre is powered by interrogation of an issue, event, and/or relationship: Why does this fifteen-year-old leave home? How can we help a victim of domestic violence overcome her predicament? The teaching artist helps participants examine questions like these, and eventually this examination results in the raising of new questions and different areas that need to be explored. In applied theatre, participants are building a future either for a character they meet

or a situation they create; there is a sense of destiny-building—a perpetual state of becoming.

7. *Applied theatre is an aesthetic medium*—Applied theatre teaching artists recognize the theatrical medium's power to place participants in situations or predicaments not readily available through alternate media. The applied theatre can entrap participants in a challenging situation that they have to work their way out of. The medium consists of an artful interplay of people, passion, and the platform as participants work toward a new, heightened, or revitalized understanding of some phenomenon.

8. *Applied theatre gives voice to communities*—Teaching artists are driven by the challenge to give voice to participants; to allow them to struggle with contradictions; to enable participants to understand how the theatre form permits us to dialogue, to interact, and to be different; and to show them how to live well in a community. Teaching artists are determined to help participants probe the multiple and shifting perspectives the applied theatre presents and are often excited by the evolving narratives participants construct.

I am at my most confident when I see an applied theatre project in which participants are permitted to dialogue, to argue, to press a point, to interrogate the logic of any given action. Divergence should be welcomed in the applied theatre because the solutions teaching artists may be inclined to make might have no greater currency or accuracy than those of the participants.

The preceding eight principles place a great deal of responsibility on the teaching artist to generate pleasing and satisfying aesthetic work that permits a sense of group ownership. In the applied theatre an aesthetic experience occurs where participants engage with the theatre form for the purpose of transformation—change. It is critical that the theatre form be sufficiently satisfying.

Facilitating Partnerships

Some years back I was involved in co-organizing an international symposium on aesthetic education that examined the critical function the artwork presents in facilitating a successful educational partnership (Taylor 2000). What does an artwork need to contain if it is to satisfy those who experience it? The applied theatre worker can deduce numerous points from the following experiences.

The three works explored at the symposium challenged the audience to interrogate the qualities of artistic praxis: "Streb," a postmodern dance; "The Divine Kiss," a multiarts contemporary opera featuring intellectually and physically challenged actors; and "Kill Everything You Love," a play about self-destruction of youths.

There was much heated conversation among symposium delegates about whether these works were artistic. I remember prominent figures in the international arts community claiming that "Streb" was merely acrobatics with a twist. Others saw different possibilities as the dancers threw themselves into walls and were catapulted into the air by rotating beams—on a human journey, as it were, to break the physical boundaries that entrap us.

It was Maxine Greene who reminded us that in aesthetic education we are seeking new perspectives and breaking with the familiar, the mundane. For Greene, the "Streb" performance made her rethink space and gravity and helped her contemplate how dancers reach beyond where they normally are, how their (our) bodies define the spaces we inhabit and the spaces we strive to reach. Greene explained that what she hopes the arts might achieve in education is a way of helping teachers and their students confront multiplicity and diversity:

> I have hopes always that if teachers are awakened, if teachers become more imaginative, if teachers face the darkness and the ambiguities of their own lives, something about what they have become may become contagious when they are in the classroom, when they are working with artists or when they are working with performances.[1]

One could equally make this claim about the teaching artist in applied theatre—they need, must, be awakened to the power of their aesthetic medium and understand the elements that power it.

---

[1]Maxine Greene expressed this view at School Reform Through the Arts, an international seminar with David Best, Maxine Greene, and Madeleine Grumet, Creative Arts Team, New York University, June 19, 1998 (see *Applied Theatre Researcher*, an electronic journal published by the Centre for Applied Theatre Research at Griffith University, at *www.gu.edu.au/centre/atr*).

At the symposium, we had similar conversations about the art-fulness of "The Divine Kiss," a visually striking piece that focused on the seven saving virtues. As actors swept toy dolls from the per-formance space, and while the audience was deluged by blinding sparks as they discovered an actor in a firestorm, I tried to fathom the significance of these images. I thought it clever of the director to cast a blind actor singing of hope on a starlit night while stand-ing beside a baby's crib and a telescope, but I wondered too about the artistic merits. And, as my doubts grew, I was again reminded of Greene (1989) who has pleaded for us to remain open to the work and that we let the images massage our senses:

> We have to realize that if we are trying to release children to be-come what they are not yet, to be free, to explore, to discover, by releasing children to move into the unknown, we can't tell them where to go—we just have to rejoice that they are alive . . . [(if)] a kind of wide-awakeness can develop through the partnership, the better chance that we have that children will wake up and rebel against dullness and boredom and repeti-tiveness and the mechanical life. I like to spend my life fighting the anaesthetic. You know, the numbness, the dullness, the re-fusal to respond to the couch-potato syndrome, so that children can see more, and feel more, and hear more, and reach further, and maybe become something more than what they call human resources for other people to mould.

Equally, the adult participants who come to the applied theatre are challenged to fight against the apathetic stance, the stance that says, "I do not care about this issue. I have no responsibility to be-come engaged in an active, community consciousness."

It was inevitable that my response to "The Divine Kiss" would be centered within my understanding of theatre form, and by how I read the seven saving virtues. Yet it was also shaped by how I read disability, by what I believe constitutes human perfection. If, as the great drama theorist Bernard Beckerman (1970) says, drama is al-ways in a state of becoming and that we who are encountering works of art are caught in situations we must work our way out of, I feel I am still trapped by "The Divine Kiss," struggling to pene-trate its layered meanings. Applied theatre works most effectively too when it entraps participants in situations where they have to struggle to make meaning, situations that demand a committed desire to unravel a mystery.

I think it is interesting that *partnership* contains within it the word *art*, p*art*nership. The most satisfying artworks, especially those found in the applied theatre, are structured so that participants interact, engage with its aesthetic possibilities, and become active participants who join with the art object. They encounter it from their own perspective based on the kinds of experiences they have had. The artwork is powered by a dynamic confrontation between the work (whether that be the object itself or the drama process) and those who experience it.

In the arts, partnerships cannot be forced and they certainly cannot be forced in applied theatre settings. Teaching artists cannot insist that participants have satisfying experiences, but they must structure the applied theatre in a way that might allow satisfaction to emerge. And knowledge of satisfaction is based on experience, education, and discipline. Experience has told us that teaching artists who take no account of their audiences, and/or who fail to acknowledge their context, might fall into some very dangerous traps. I was heartened to hear Irish author Roddy Doyle, on an English interview show, say that his primary concern as a high school teacher for twelve years was to keep the students interested—to entertain them if you like (Merkin 1999). Which made me think of the British educator Dorothy Heathcote who, we are told, pioneered the teacher-in-role strategy initially because she needed to focus her students' attention and thought she could do that most effectively by shaping the form and content from within the drama. Thus, a new teaching technique emerged from experience (in Bolton 2003).

Often, the most effective teaching artists are able to see themselves as working in partnership with their stakeholders. Cecily O'Neill (1995) uses the perceptive image of effective teaching artists as those who are able to lead the way while walking backward. She argues that leaders need to act as guides who should know where the travelers have come from, and the nature of the journey so far, so that they can help shape the kind of journey that lies ahead. Rather than leading with their backs to the participants, leaders face them while moving forward, conscious of where the group is at and what they are capable of achieving. *Walking back-*

ward to the future is a delightful metaphor for describing good applied theatre partnerships.

Avoid the deadly applied theatre programs in which outcomes are known in advance and a kind of leader-dictation lesson emerges, a situation where participants merely jump through the teaching artist's hoops. Teaching artists would do well to follow the models inspired by many of the great drama educators (see Heinemann's Dimensions of Drama Series).[2] Teaching artists in the applied theatre and drama education have not always been educated to construe their praxis in this manner; the next section briefly highlights pedagogical approaches to avoid.

AN APPLIED THEATRE TEACHING ARTIST STANCE TO AVOID

Many teaching artists in the applied theatre come from a range of different educational backgrounds where they have learned models of teaching that might not hold up to scrutiny today. Here I discuss one model, which very much influenced me and which I discovered some years later might not be as effective as I thought for building successful partnerships in the applied theatre.

I well recall my own early years as a seventh-grade drama student. The classroom of the early 1970s was characterized by a different conception of the teaching artist from that which O'Neill suggests and I promote in this book. Picture, if you will, a classroom isolated from the main school building—a portable room separated from the other teaching spaces. As the children enter this blacked-out space, they notice a figure standing by the stereo system, assorting and selecting records. This teacher looked like he might have just come from a hippie commune, adorned as he was with beads while the kaleidoscopic patterns on his outfit seem to beckon the students in.

"Come in and get ready, my treasures," the teacher said, as my classmates and I enthusiastically prepared ourselves, changing into

---

[2]The Dimensions of Drama Series addresses issues of effective praxis (action, reflection, transformation) and research in drama and theatre education. The praxis outlined in this series resembles that required from the applied theatre teaching artist.

our free-flowing gear, removing our shoes, going through the required rituals as we prepared for drama.

"Now, find your own space and lie down," he added, fascinated
by the record sleeves he was holding, meticulously taking each one
out of the box and contemplating its dramatic possibilities. And
so we would separate around the room, eager to begin the familiar
routine of our drama class.

"Okay, now focus on your breathing, center those breaths.
Hands on your diaphragm." He would walk around the room. "Eyes
shut now, settle down. Concentrate." Concentrate was the common instruction of the 1970s. We had this view that the drama
teacher was the expert, a mystical figure what's more, whose soft
and gently spoken instructions we would willingly obey.

"Now, imagine you are lying on a beach. My, the sun feels good
doesn't it, as it massages your body?" As the students enjoyed the
sensations, the teacher provided an affirming comment, "You feel
like you are sinking through the sand, you are so relaxed."

Little did we know that the restful and soothing nature of our
contemplations was soon to be horribly transformed. "The sun is
now wrenching hot, and you feel your body starting to sweat all
over," the teacher said sternly. "You are grossly uncomfortable as
you try and fight your way out of this suffocation but, oh no," he
quickly added, "someone has shackled your ankles and wrists, you
can't move. You scream for help, but you have no voice."

As our anxiety grew and our bodies gyrated with all the inten-
sity of people who have been trapped against their will, the teacher
finally said, "And the shackles are removed. Relax. Feel yourself
sinking again. Center your breathing, in, then out." After a minute
or so we were told to sit up in our own time—"In your own time"
was a frequent teacher directive as well.

We begin to see in this model how the leader pursues a complete participant-submersion policy. He instructs participants how
to respond and they dutifully follow the instructions. This model
in the applied theatre would not promote participant autonomy
but rather a mindless state in which instructions must be obeyed.

"Come over to me," he then waved, "and listen attentively." He
had selected the record to play—"Peter and the Wolf," a particular favorite, old but definitely still popular in the early 1970s. He

said, "I want you to imagine that you are going on a trip through the magical forest. You must first get ready, pack your bags, get your supplies together." And, as we mimicked getting ready for an adventure, our teacher, noticeably happy with our efforts, added, "We are now ready for our journey."

Then we enacted the teacher's narrative of going through the forest while the selected music served as a backdrop. He reminded us that in this particular setting we were likely to come across the most amazing creatures, "Each more amazing with every turn along the forest's path." As readers can imagine, we demonstrated the appropriate emotions at the required sections: fear, relief, and joy being just three of them.

The notion that the work must pursue one linear narrative was common in those days, but what consequently emerged was a group of mimicking nonthinking participants incapable of realizing their own possibilities and hopes during the work. We have seen that applied theatre requires a more critical stance from the participants, a stance where opportunities for them to pose suggestions, raise alternatives, co-construct their own narrative or version of events are provided throughout.

Now, the major theme of the session was introduced, usually the theme focused on a popular issue like advertising; a lot of the work in the seventies was issue-based. As the teacher shared magazine pages about how companies marketed their products with us, we became amused at the familiar ploys of advertisers to gain our attention: the sparkling smiling white teeth for a new brand of toothpaste, the conventional nuclear family munching on their healthy breakfast, the slim attractive couple in their new denim jeans.

Our task for the lesson was to work in small groups and incorporate some of these devices into a television commercial to market a new product. Yes, highly entertaining for participants and audience. On a good day, all of the groupwork was shared and our lesson would close with another relaxation exercise, usually lying on the floor with our breathing being the focus. My teacher was always concerned that we demonstrate the appropriate signals of being relaxed, which meant that our palms had to be facing up. He knew we weren't relaxed if, when he came to lift our arms, they were not limp. "You're not relaxed," he would note, unhappily, to the offenders.

Not long ago, I remember describing this familiar 1970s drama class experience for a large group of educators at a conference, and being rebuked by a group of three women for satirizing their own pedagogy. Clearly, such a pattern is still in evidence today. Although I do not want to undermine this style of teaching, it is difficult to characterize this way of working as a partnership between educators and participants. Teachers, it seems, did not necessarily see themselves as being partnered with their students in the seventies. Likewise, there has been a critique of the applied theatre teaching artist leading participants through an uninspired, nonnegotiable sequence of illogical activities (Jackson 1993; see Swortzell chapter).

In Bolton's 1979 book, *Towards a Theory of Drama in Education*, he deconstructs this kind of education and how it was motivated by having participants mindlessly pursue the dictated steps of the leader. One problem with this lesson is that there is no logic to it, the bits are not coherently linked. In some respects, this style of teaching reminds me of the well-oiled aerobics lesson, popular in the 1980s, which, ironically, I was very much into at the time. Common to both, we have the familiar warm up. In the drama class, it included stock physical exercises, which became predictable after some time, but movement and voice exercises were the staple. Head rolls, for example, were popular, even in the aerobics class I might add.

The main activity in the aerobics lesson would be the intense cardiovascular workout, which included lots of jumping and running. In the drama class, we were usually divided into groups that then made up miniplays based on stimulus materials given by the teacher. The closure of the drama class, called the cool down in aerobics, included numerous relaxation exercises, again dictated by the leader. Just as Bolton argues how flawed this kind of structure can be, it is interesting that by the end of the 1980s fitness groups distanced themselves from the ankle-jarring, bone-crushing routines of the typical aerobics session, preferring more low-impact workouts, which were seen as less physically damaging. Head rolls, for instance, we had learned can cause considerable damage to people's necks if not executed correctly. I am still troubled today when I observe intense, harmful physical warm-up routines in drama classes.

Just as there is little in the way of joint sharing between teachers and their participants in this praxis, there is little partnering between the gym instructor and the client. Although signs of seventies' teaching are still evident, the field of theatre education has moved on considerably as it now incorporates the voices and minds of all participants. Common sense suggests that individuals are more likely to feel committed to the drama lesson process and the applied theatre when they are actively involved in initiating and shaping the content and form.

In applied theatre, the teaching artists must avoid the errors of the drama educators of the 1970s when autocrats ruled classrooms and participants were merely guinea pigs—virtual laboratory fodder for the leader. "Just put yourselves into my hands," the leader suggested, "and I promise you that a great experience will be had." Partnerships built on notions of expertise limit the control participants have when collaborating with teaching artists. There are real dangers when participants put themselves in the teaching artists' hands and believe in a false sense of security based on faith. Teaching artists must embrace a collegial and collaborative model in which there is a recognition that their outlook on life also can be changed by the participants. The praxis of applied theatre recognizes that while the teaching artist is an informed leader, the created work demands the input and control of all those involved with it.

In innovative partnerships, participants should join with their teaching artists and share their knowledge, and in doing so gain a sense of increased power. We must work against traditional environments' dominant model, where participants are satisfied that their interests are being looked after and that they need only comply with the advice of their leaders for all to be well. It can be educationally damaging if we perpetuate the notion that experts will look after us—experts can be wrong and can lead us astray.

In innovative partnerships, all parties should exercise control over the situation. A camaraderie is forged among teaching artists and participants as they work together, acting as mutual collaborators. As Freire (1970) argues, when teachers can engage in authentic dialogue with students, the students become self-reliant and a more equitable sharing of power emerges:

> [T]he teacher-of-the-students and the students-of-the-teacher cease to exist and a new term emerges: teacher–student with student–teacher. The teacher is no longer merely the one who teaches, but one who is himself taught in dialogue with the students, who, in their turn, while being taught, also teach. (67)

I would argue that in applied theatre the same occurs: the teaching artist can learn just as much from the participants, and vice versa. So the teaching artist is not merely the one who leads, but one who is equally led by participants. Aims are negotiated and transformed in progress and predicted outcomes are no longer the focus. Good praxis in applied theatre works toward a joint partnership in which knowledge, talents, and skills are shared.

THE FACILITATOR'S AMBITION—ACTION, REFLECTION, TRANSFORMATION

In the applied theatre, teaching artists' greatest strength lies in their ability to help participants develop a relationship with the work. In many instances, when participants come to the applied theatre, they might be skeptical of the program's nature, or suspect the motivations of the applied theatre team. Teaching artists might be viewed as an instrument of the state, the authorized pedagogue who summons the people and tells them how they should behave and think. As demonstrated in past research in the theatre for development (TfD) movement, applied theatre can often fall into a *Father Knows Best* attitude—a clear arrogance on the part of the commissioning body in the selection of issues to be examined (Ahmed 2002):

> These issues supposedly come from the people themselves. However, as the process of play-making shows, the issues are selected by the village co-ordination committee, the union co-ordination committee or the troupe and each play projects a clear top-down message. Hence, there is little room for Freirean "dialogue" with the spectators or for the performers to act as a Boalian "forum." (211)

What seems to be a true negotiation is often not; key pedagogical decisions are made before participants are genuinely engaged with the work. Readers will see echoes here with the practice in many drama education classrooms described earlier wherein the pedagogical approach was one driven by monologist renderings of human affairs rather than dialogic ones.

The facilitator in the applied theatre has to be genuinely committed to engaging participants in a dialogue, a dialogue which recognizes that change has to be driven from within the community. Otherwise, as Mda (in Pompeo-Nogueira 2002) confirms, participants are cornered into being the mere receivers of a preordained message and are powerless to actively sharpen their ability to interpret, to dispute, to believe in their own worth to decide what material is and is not worth interrogating:

> The superior external agent decides, solely on technical grounds, how best to solve the problem in the villages and devises his own plans to facilitate the solution. No attempt is made to consult villagers before the plans are formulated.

The applied theatre poses many challenges because teaching artists are not delivering a prepackaged curriculum, but are working in unison with participants to assist them to build a critical consciousness. The teaching artist needs to learn how to facilitate, when to ask probing questions, and how to allow participants' responses to speak for themselves. The facilitator needs to encourage, to coax, participants to enter the imaginary world and to help them feel protected and not presented as the laughing stock to a raucous audience of bemused admirers.

The facilitator is not merely the one who asks questions, or who initiates tasks, but someone who shares with the participants versions of how she or he as the teaching artist is responding to the evolving work. While facilitators must not be seen as too value-laden, or to lack clear objectivity, they need to learn the delicate skills of being able to voice their own perspective—their understanding—of what is possible and what is not.

The facilitator should work with participants rather than against them. Although I do sympathize with the views of critics of the Boalian theatre who question the facilitators' motivations, one would hope that any attempt to engage communities in a struggle to critique the nature of their world and their place in it is far better than a status quo stance that condones oppression and people's powerlessness (O'Sullivan 2001).

In each of the examples of the applied theatre in this book, readers will note how the teaching artists act as negotiators who liaise between the individuals and a desire to empower participants to voice their own relationship to the issues or events under consideration. As I write these words, I am well aware of how difficult it is for facilitators to permit participants to experience their own reading of the applied theatre when the work is often commissioned by external agencies for the sole purpose of "inducting" groups into a particular worldview (e.g., vandalism is wrong, or alarming increases in teenage suicide and pregnancy must be stopped).

The critical issue for the facilitator is not to divorce the partnerships from the context in which they occur. There are huge risks involved for applied theatre facilitators when they enter communities believing they can effect change. The most one can hope for is to engage the community in a dialogue and with a presentation so that all participants can interact with the focused area. Facilitators need to consider the extent to which the questions applied theatre poses resonate with the immediate community concerns.

Facilitators are most likely to produce significant work in applied theatre when they *activate* the dual artist–educator role; *reflect* on their own contribution to the applied theatre partnership; and *transform* understandings of the participants' worldview.

Facilitators Activate the Artist–Educator Role

It seems appropriate to begin this section with a quotation from the illuminating American educator, historian, and philosopher Maxine Greene (1978). Greene has devoted much of her professional career to promoting what she describes as wide-awakeness, an alert state of consciousness in which individuals reflect on the world and the role they play in it.

> So many of us today confine ourselves to right angles. We function in the narrowest of specialties; we lead one-dimensional lives. We accommodate ourselves so easily to the demands of the technological society—to time schedules, charts, programs, techniques—that we lose touch with our streams of consciousness, our inner time. (198–99)

Greene's concern is that educators reluctantly become strangers to their own practice. Professional growth, she asserts, is located in teaching artists' ability to revisit their work with renewed eyes and possibly transform themselves through a deliberate and critical self-examination of their own fallible pedagogy. It is perhaps no surprise to learn of Greene's indebtness to John Dewey and his championing of the individual's capacity to remind oneself to reconsider, to stop, to pause, to meditate, and to contemplate an issue or phenomenon in a different way and thereby provoke an enlightened perspective.

There is clearly a contradiction between raising participants' consciousness and delivering an external *top-down* program. Inevitably, the odds are against participants assuming the stance of knowledgeable individuals capable of reflective thought and assuming responsibility for their lives when authoritative others have been charged with this responsibility.

But common sense dictates that if the participants depend on others to do their thinking for them, they may develop a sense of hopelessness and are potentially condemned to isolation and despair. In a book about the role of critical pedagogy in our daily lives, Clar Doyle (1993) claims that education is not a neutral process and cannot be denuded of the social, human, and historical elements that make up the process of teaching. Educators, he suggests, have not always been willing to account for their own and their students' "socially determined taste, prior knowledge, language forms, abilities and modes of knowing" (83). I would argue that the applied theatre facilitator needs to question the ideologies that power their own praxis.

For instance, although there has been much interest in the rise of the TfD movement, this interest sometimes is championed by privileged Western democracies where the interests of the middle class are firmly secured. Facilitators need to be conscious of their own values and to understand how these might be read by the communities in which they work. Both Doyle and Greene remind us that learning is affected by its own cultural milieu. Each educational event is powered by an array of cultural and particular ethnic biases. Teaching artists, then, need to activate their own ability to think, assess, and reassess within the communities where applied theatre happens.

Facilitators Reflect

The playwright and drama critic Bertolt Brecht was concerned with developing techniques to distance the spectator from the action if the dramatic work was to get the audience to consider the truths of their world (Willett 1977). Facilitators in the applied theatre need to find similar distancing strategies to examine their praxis. Clearly, facilitators need to become reflective practitioners.

The term *reflective practitioner* has been widely promoted in the field of architectural design by Donald Schön (1983). It is sometimes referred to as teacher-research, critical pedagogy, or action research, although each labeling has its own histories and emphases. Reflective practitioners empower themselves to contemplate critically some aspect of their own teaching and learning processes. They tend to be suspicious of educational and curriculum documents that have not been grounded in and powered by actual experiences. Reflective practitioners are interested in searching for themes in the communities in which they work to question how these themes directly inform their immediate and ongoing praxis.

To be an effective facilitator in applied theatre is to be a reflective practitioner. Both facilitators and reflective practitioners give birth to ideas and both search for a medium to express and honor their visions. Like reflective practitioners, teaching artists (according to Greene 1989, 216)

> are for disclosing the extraordinary in the ordinary. They are for transfiguring the commonplace, as they embody their perceptions and feelings and understandings in a range of languages, in formed substance of many kinds. They are for affirming the work of imagination—the cognitive capacity that summons up the "as-if," the possible, the what is not and yet what might be. They are for doing all this in such a way as to enable those who open themselves to what they create to see more, to hear more, to feel more, to attend to more facets of the experienced world.

For participants to have an experience in applied theatre, they need to project themselves into the work—they need to encounter it and allow it to speak to them. I am reminded how, in my own life, the most powerful encounters I have had with applied theatre are those in which I have had an internal conversation between the work and myself.

Facilitators are sometimes trapped by the external requirements placed on them by their funders, by their directors, by the organizations in which they work. Rather than facilitators being arrested by the moment—by *What is happening now?*—they are driven by *What is happening next?* We all can recognize a facilitator who asks that question: What is happening next? They move through the program as if it were a discrete body of information that needs to be digested by participants. They are governed by endpoints—the end of the activity, the time clock, the questions they wrote down in advance.

If such facilitators were to ask participants a different kind of question rather than the *next* but *now* ones, they would be challenging an investigation of the moment, catching participants up in the here and now. Previous chapters provide examples of how the work can be held up by participants and how it can be scrutinized so that facilitators can critically ponder what the work is or is not demonstrating. Unfortunately, however, many of the circumstances in which applied theatre happens can work against the here and now because of the performance of preordained tasks and the completion of prescribed attainment tasks and activities.

The most effective facilitators are able to reflect on the kind of teaching artists they are and the possible ones they can become. Reflection, though, requires distance. As participants gain distance, they can begin to see how the work operates. They, like good artists, can evaluate the created work. If participants are going to learn anything from their encounters with applied theatre, they need to have a conversation with facilitators through and about it so that facilitators can help participants represent their own vision of their world. Facilitators join with the participants and become spect-actors who actively work together to construct meaning.

Applied theatre reconstructs and interrogates a portrait of the times in which we live. Operating well, applied theatre enables participants to commit to its format and to reflect on themselves and their world. In other words, like Boal's spect-actors (Boal 1995), they ask *What is happening to me now?*; spect-actors are always asking it as they begin to dialogue with the applied theatre.

Facilitators Transform

Teaching artists must not lose sight of the power of the art form to transform, to move, and to shift. I am thinking here of the existential experience—the lived moment, the encounter between what is created and what is perceived. This poses some real dilemmas for facilitators.

Good applied theatre aims to devise roles and situations that explore the human condition, not as a way of answering the problems of the world but to help develop a perspective on the world and to understand or at least struggle with the perspectives of others as we move toward a sense of social justice and equity. Applied theatre enables participants to struggle with the contradictions, to work through a dilemma, to interpret the lives of people under stress.

As the previous section argues, applied theatre operates as a reflective encounter, but simultaneously it is a transformative encounter that can help change or alter human perceptions of the world. At the very least, applied theatre should leave participants with good questions they can take away with them.

Like great works of art, applied theatre shares a mission to transform. We can all think of examples in which a performance, an exhibition, a recital has unnerved us, leaving us with a slight sense of unease or an uncomfortable yet necessary disturbance; in other words, an artistic event that has generated more questions than it answers. An event from my own experience might help clarify this.

When I saw a performance of the Vineyard Theatre's Manhattan production of Paula Vogel's play, "How I Learned to Drive," I was reminded of the integral connection between art and education. In Vogel's play, the unsettling questions focus on sexual awakening. The play raises unnerving issues about child sexual abuse and the audience's, perhaps unknown, complicity in such events. The play focuses on Li'l Bit, a woman who, we are told, ages "forty something" to eleven years old. The play is a series of reflections on Li'l Bit's life, and as her story unfolds and we witness the relationship that develops between her and her Uncle Peck, our response is not simply one of outrage but of uncertainty as we struggle with the complex portraits of the characters' lives.

"How I Learned to Drive" is told, in part, through the eyes of a Greek Chorus, a device I'm sure Vogel selected so that the audience could be further distanced from the events in order to understand them more fully. The Greek Chorus assumes various roles and situations that surround Li'l Bit and Uncle Peck. And as the Chorus demonstrates their various parts, we project our own lives into those displayed before us, seeing our frailties, passions, hopes, and dreams.

Toward the end of the play, one Greek Chorus member assumes the character of Aunt Mary, Uncle Peck's wife. Aunt Mary is a complex woman. She loves her husband, knows that he has a personality that is, for want of a better term, on the edge. At the same time, she is a confused woman who looks for scapegoats and deflects responsibility from herself and Peck onto others.

> My husband was such a good man—is. Is such a good man. Every night, he does the dishes. The second he comes home, he's taking out the garbage, or doing yard work, lifting the heavy things I can't. Everyone in the neighborhood borrows Peck . . .

Then later she adds (1998):

> And I want to say this about my niece. She's a sly one, that one is. She knows exactly what she's doing; she's twisted Peck around her little finger and thinks it's all a big secret. Yet another one who's borrowing my husband until it doesn't suit her anymore.
>
> Well. I'm counting the days until she goes away to school. And she manipulates someone else. And then he'll come back again, and sit in the kitchen while I bake, or beside me on the sofa when I sew in the evenings. I'm a very patient woman. But I'd like my husband back.
>
> I'm counting the days. (66–67)

And when she finished with those words, "I am counting the days," I reflected on the kind of compromises that woman has made, and the costs of such compromises on herself and those around her; I wondered to what extent I too close myself off to reality, ignoring the pain, the inhumanity, and the suffering that surrounds me. How often do I blame the Li'l Bits of this world for others' failings? Vogel unnerves us because we have to project ourselves into the work if it is to reach us. And maybe, if it is to fully reach us, we need to locate aspects of Aunt Mary, of Li'l Bit, and maybe even of Uncle Peck that exist in ourselves.

If by the word *educate* we mean there is a need to help others search, to draw them out, to raise their level of consciousness and insight, to question and probe, "How I Learned to Drive" fulfills the criterion of an educative work. But it too is an artwork, a subtly rendered work, which operates through the imagination, through a metaphor if you like, that permits contemplative and reflective thought.

Facilitators need to understand how the aesthetic medium works as a transformative encounter. They have at their fingers a powerful medium but if managed poorly, they may well undermine its power. To a certain extent, the success of an applied theatre program rests on the facilitators' shoulders. They are the ones implementing the work with their fellow teaching artists; with the participants; with the wider communities in which the work is presented; with the funding agencies, administrators, and officials. Ultimately, if teaching artists are to find ways of helping participants commit to the program, they need to manage their work in partnership with these vested interests.

IN CLOSING: ARTISTRY AND FACILITATION

I can identify six characteristics that teaching artists in the applied theatre need to develop if they are to become effective facilitators. Readers will note an overlap here with many of the principles of applied theatre outlined in the Introduction.

1. *Critical thinkers*—Rather than accepting designed programs at face value, facilitators are sensitive to the historical, political, and social contexts that power the applied theatre. They are suspicious about simply "consuming" the values, attitudes, and ideas of others. They recognize that the informed teaching artist must understand how each segment of the applied theatre program has been constructed and whose interests it serves.

2. *Risk takers*—Following the crowd can be easier than standing alone. Facilitators recognize the difficulties in activating their communities as sites of critical inquiry but know that their role is

to challenge mainstream discourses and to find alternate ways to help participants change current predicaments.

3. *Theory generators*—Based on direct observation of the contexts for applied theatre, facilitators develop informed programs based on direct participant observation. The applied theatre programs are designed in partnership with the communities in which they are to be experienced.

4. *Open-minded and flexible*—Facilitators try to develop multiple perspectives on particular events. They must be sensitive to different voices and capable of "rethinking" cherished ideas. When attempting a new approach or responding to immediate demands, we are often liable to make errors. Facilitators understand that success can come through perceived failure.

5. *Collaborative*—Facilitators recognize that they do not work alone. They engage their participants, their fellow teaching artists, their colleagues, their funders and benefactors, the administrators, and the wider community in their endeavor to create powerful applied theatre programs. Facilitators are aware that strategies and program content appropriate in one setting may not be appropriate in another.

6. *Storytellers*—Facilitators listen and respond to their own stories and to ones of those with whom they work. Communities become sites for storytelling, story-responding, and story-creating. Facilitators must not be afraid of putting their stories up for interrogation, but they must ensure that they do not overpower. All voices need to be heard.

4

THE ETHICS OF
APPLIED THEATRE

Now that we have begun to isolate the characteristics of the applied theatre and the demands placed on the teaching artists who help make it happen, an ethical question should be addressed: *Is applied theatre moral?* By the word *moral*, I mean the underlying humane values informing the choices and the implementations of the programs teaching artists and funding bodies make. Are these values inspired by a sense of duty and moral imperative? Might applied theatre be motivated by some superior urge to have community members conform to a mainstream standard, or for them to behave according to a preordained policy? Whose standards is the applied theatre enforcing? How do these standards interface with the communities who experience applied theatre?

I am fascinated by these questions, which often get to the heart of who has the power and how this power is wielded. The questions are not any different from those good educators ask themselves every day as they make decisions about which material to focus on, the values powering that material, and how to assist participants engage with the material.

This chapter "unpacks" some of the ethical dilemmas applied theatre workers inevitably find themselves in, and the ways they can design and implement work that genuinely seeks a meeting of different moral positions. I am particularly interested in examining work that encourages participants to put their stories up for scrutiny. When rendering people's life stories into the dramatic medium, must certain confidentialities and assurances be given? If so, as a matter of policy and principle, do applied theatre workers provide these assurances? What dilemmas do these programs place applied theatre workers in, and how are the commissioning agents responding to the dilemmas?

We are discovering how often applied theatre is a political theatre, indebted to the formative praxis of Brecht and Boal. It can be a confrontational medium because it places participants in situations that might require them to challenge injustices, to speak freely, to agitate for change. Applied theatre involves a community-building ethic whereby people come together to act, to reflect, to transform. Sometimes applied theatre workers draw on techniques embraced by the avant-garde as a way to highlight or confront some disturbing developments in human relations. Characters might not speak in linear sentences, narratives might be shattered, discomforting images might be revealed, worlds might be in disarray. Because of participants' personal involvement, which applied theatre demands, it can raise emotions, expose insecurities, and lead to heated exchanges. Should raising emotions be a purpose of the applied theatre?

Sometimes applied theatre manufactures challenging scenarios in order to get a response from participants. A program focused on homophobia, for instance, might ask participants to project themselves into the role of the victim of a hate crime—one who is tormented and vilified by the community. Applied theatre might leave participants with more questions than answers. Participants might emerge from the homophobia program not knowing how to prevent such incidents or they might be unsure whether the actions they have taken were credible. When participants are "entrapped" within an applied theatre program and find themselves employed in the situations being played out in front of them, do the teaching artists have a particular responsibility to protect participants from getting too emotionally caught up in the material? Just as there are responsibilities on researchers when they enter communities and document the lived experience of those they observe, are similar demands placed on teaching artists? What makes applied theatre an ethical theatre?

If we accept that applied theatre is usually, if not always, taking place in a field setting, do the teaching artists liken themselves to qualitative inquirers gathering and analyzing data? How can we be assured that those who write up reports of fieldwork have presented accurate or authentic depictions of life in the field? Should we really care if these descriptions are trustworthy? These questions point to the permissions sought by the applied theatre stakeholders to work with a range of community groups. They also highlight the integrity with which the stories are told, shaped, and interrogated. When authors describe their experiences in a range of applied theatre communities in written reports, are they compelled to include caveats that the stories they tell have been authenticated by those who participated in the program?

THE CHALLENGES

In the theatre for development (TfD) movement, for instance, we are reading about an ever-increasing incidence of community theatre programs that are grassroots driven. The hallmark of TfD has been a documented insistence that community members actively negotiate the content and execution of the work at every phase of its evolution. Supposedly, this presumes that a bottom-up process is powering TfD (Ogolla Nyangore 2000):

> TfD recognizes and deals with problems of direct relevance to a people' socio-economic realities; it is culturally relevant and inexpensive. It also dissolves the artist–audience boundary by stimulating discussion and dialogue on the issues of the performance, bridging the communication gap between project initiators and recipients to make the project understandable and acceptable to the people. (79)

Contained within this description is a celebration of the equitable and the negotiable. While one should celebrate notions of equity and justice, it is imperative that the applied theatre teaching artist ask *Who is the project serving?* When projects are being commissioned by outside agents who have their own criteria and rationale for presenting the program, there could be an implied conflict of agendas. What one can find informing the projects' descriptions in some TfD are implications that the teaching artists are merely the instrument of an external agenda. The teaching artists are not generating new material but merely recycling the dictum of a government or other authoritative agency.

In one project, Ogolla Nyangore describes how a local water supply agency commissioned a theatre troupe to develop a program for the purpose of transmitting knowledge about proper hygiene. The water and sanitation messages the project needed to transmit included indoctrination about using a latrine and the need to "wash hands after using the latrine" (2000, 79). Here, we see the TfD teaching artists delivering what might be considered formal knowledge—the important facts to ensure, in their view, a healthy community lifestyle. Theatre is being used for a most didactic purpose: to inform the community members to wash their hands after they use the toilet. One might ask whether this is indeed the most appropriate engagement for the theatre form; others would argue that theatre is able to teach such facts more effectively than any other medium.

In this particular project, the commissioning agent is clearly identified as are the concerns the TfD workers had about the project. Hinting at the misuse of theatre within developing communities, Ogolla Nyangore asks: "How can we ensure that the persuasive power of theatre is not used for transmitting messages far less beneficial to the community?" (84). It is clear that if commissioning agents understand the power of theatre as a teaching tool, they could well entice troupes to create programs for propaganda reasons or to sway public opinion to a number of subversive causes.

Gaining Distance

In a different program, which does not aim to transmit a fact or to preach an outcome, a team of dedicated outreach theatre workers research, design, and implement a work about sex abuse. The outreach theatre program developed by a university department aims to permit adult survivors of child abuse to air their grievances, especially their sense of betrayal by their mothers (Dobson, Goode, & Boyd, 2000). Here the teaching artists are placed in an immediate dilemma: How can I deal with this volatile and potentially explosive issue in a protective and supportive manner? Because the material they are dealing with is loaded with hateful and shocking memories so directly connected to the participants' real lives, it is of genuine concern that the program might place them in too emotional a state. The artists ponder whether they are dipping too deeply into territory better dealt with by the therapist. They search for a fictitious situation that will permit the group to explore child abuse while not positioning the members in roles in which they will have to directly play out the actual circumstances of their lives.

They seek an analogous moment and they search for a distanced role. During the preliminary workshops with the survivors, the women's betrayal by their mothers emerged as a strong theme. Believing that this theme could serve as the basis for a performance piece with the women, the teaching artists generate scenarios, which hold strong resonance with the experiences of others. Based on the work with the women, the artists constructed a character, Shelly, a victim of child abuse. Shelly is not the name of a real person in the group, nor does she represent one person's story; she became an amalgam, a virtual pastiche powered by the stories of many. Shelly is a narrative in the making, comprised of multiple vignettes from the group. The more representative Shelly is of the whole group's story, the more likely participants can commit to her.

When a teddy bear was brought into the workshop environment, it was seen as a protective device for the outreach theatre. The teddy bear would permit the women to create a context for exploration. Dolls and objects have been widely used in therapy sessions for clients to vent or reveal their inner self. In this project, the toy bear serves a similar purpose, releasing participants to act out fictitious scenarios based on real events.

Participants construct a scene in which Shelly, in role as the bear's mother, speaks to the toy (Dobson, Goode, & Boyd 2000):

> I can't be here to cuddle you all the time so you're going to have to learn to stick up for yourself. That is your box, and you have to stay there good and clean, washed and nice for people to see you. I am your mummy, but I can only look after you sometimes. I am very busy with the cooking and the cleaning and I've got all my other babies to look after. (194)

From this dialogue between the teddy bear and Shelly, "the maximum possible emotional distance between the fiction and past reality" enables the participants to explore notions of loss and betrayal. "The survivors are condensing their own life experiences," argue Dobson and his colleagues, "to create Shelly as a fictional other" (195). Shelly becomes a composite representation of the survivors and her interactions with the teddy bear lead them to more fully explore the nature of their lives, their sense of victimhood, their sense of survival.

Through the role-playing with the teddy bear, participants are able to grapple with the demons from their past as they process a positive future for themselves. We learn that these workshops with people who suffered betrayal in their lives can become the basis for a one-person play on abuse. In this program, we witness teaching artists' work from a "committed sense of their own social responsibility and accountability" as they create a "one woman performance piece which would offer a perspective on abuse" (189–198).

Teaching artists strongly believe in the power of the theatre art form to create situations and protected moments that enable participants to interrogate their past and present lives as they begin to build a successful future. The artists draw on the stories of real people as they construct their program. Shelly though becomes the fictitious means through which participants can project themselves into the work and begin, with the artists' help, a process of discovery, healing, and education.

The participants then engaged in a series of exercises, not at all dissimilar from the ones previously described in this text, in which they can reclaim Shelly's lost childhood. For instance, her dreams and ambitions are demonstrated through the creation of a series of physical representations, what Boal (1995) describes as *image theatre*. These representations of the protagonists' desire are deconstructed by the group and their qualities are canvassed as participants reflect on the various images.

In building a future for Shelly, participants are constructing a narrative for themselves so that they can interrogate how the negative experiences of their formative years can be transformed. Shelly becomes the vehicle through which participants' own ambitions are presented. "This was liberating for the women," according to Dobson et al., "who felt that it was possible to hope and dream within the fictional world in ways that had been impossible for them in reality" (196). The imaginary world becomes a potent medium for participants to explore the real world; rather than the applied theatre being an escape, it is grounded in real-life experiences.

Clearly, the challenge for these artists was to process the painful stories of the women survivors in a way that would enable them to share their past in order to build a positive future. Although it is unclear from the published account of the work how the teaching artists gained access to the women and what kind of release forms were presented, the book chapter provides us with a probing account of how an applied theatre project is devised with the participants to help them explore issues that relate to their abuse.

Getting Closer

In the project just described, the teaching artists believed that emotional distance was critical to the applied theatre. In applied theatre, teaching artists are often sensitive to maintaining psychological distance so that too strong an emotional response from participants can be curbed. This concern is one shared in the broader field of drama in education; there has been a reluctance to set up situations that place participants in events likely to arouse feelings that are too deep. It would be unlikely, for example, for a drama educator to reenact a scene of child abuse, incest, rape, or some other shocking crime. Sexism, ageism, racism, and homophobia themes can be dealt with better by finding roles and situations that do not too directly mirror actual events.

The drama educators steer away from structuring episodes that will generate powerful emotional responses from participants. Scenes that might be too painful can be dealt with through an analogy, or by finding a distanced frame of reference where connections to real-life incidents are made through indirect observation or, perhaps, a culminating discussion. Going on a mission to outer space and finding a planet where people with blue eyes are isolated from others might serve as the basis for a project on discrimination. A select group of scientists working on a cloning experiment with dogs might serve as a drama about survival of the fittest, and what human breeds are more desirable than others!

It is unlikely that a drama educator interested in a project about how gross sexual abuse to a minor can occur would set up a situation where an eight-year-old girl's body is found bound, naked, and decomposed in a remote area and have participants attempt to construct a profile of a person who might commit such an act. Educators interested in work on the deviant mind might use Edgar Allen

Poe's "The Tell Tale Heart" (1979) as the pre-text for an exploration of how the protagonist in that story felt compelled to rid himself of an old man's "evil eye." If parallels are to be made to more contemporary situations, these would be done through inference. Distance and protection are two qualities often sought for in drama education.

Nevertheless, these concerns are not always shared by therapists and counselors who use theatre to examine issues related to self-identity. There can be an interesting difference between how the drama therapist and the applied theatre artist operate. The drama therapist is interested in rebuilding a self, often a shattered/broken self, and aims to explore how participants/clients can more ably negotiate the circumstances of their lives. There is a therapeutic imperative to this mission—drama processes are intentionally used to alleviate psychological and physical stress. The client engages the therapist for this very purpose. Distinguished drama therapist Robert Landy (1993) argues that the objectives of drama therapy are to "increase one's role repertory, and to learn how to play a single role more spontaneously and competently" (233).

People who have experienced some major personal crisis—loss of a loved one, an emotional breakdown, dependence on drugs and/or alcohol, chronic illness—have sometimes surrendered confidence in their ability to cope with conflicts or are at a loss to know how to manage their depressions and/or anxieties. Drama therapists use the art form as a way of reliving, perhaps, but also processing and probing the events and moments that have so negatively impacted on their clients' ability to operate effectively in the world.

These interests were certainly evident at a marriage therapy session where drama techniques were used to help a client reflect on her life (Nolte 2000). Following two years of marriage, a young woman identified as Suzanne consults a therapist to find out why her relationship seems to be falling apart. Through a sequence of guided questions, the therapist asks Suzanne to reenact moments from her childhood. She acts out her life as a seven-year-old in the bath playing with her toys when she hears a fight downstairs between her mother and her sister; it appears physical abuse was involved during the fight. This argument is recreated with Suzanne in role as her mother screaming at Suzanne's sister, another participant in role: "I wish you were never born, you damn brat! I hate you! I hate you!" (213).

From this role-play emerges the fact that Suzanne's sister was seeking her help during the encounter. "I don't know what to do," explains Suzanne during this therapy session, "Theresa is calling for help and nobody else is going to help her. I don't want to go. Mother will hit me too" (214). During the therapy session, Suzanne is reliving a memory of how she felt manipulated by family members when she was growing up. The session reveals that Suzanne had a complex, difficult relationship with her mother and often felt placed in the middle of arguments between her mother and her sister. Suzanne constantly felt she was the peacemaker who was trying to satisfy the needs of others. Emotional scenes are then played out in which seven-year-old Suzanne ends up in tears in the family home. One poignant moment has Suzanne kneeling with her head in her mother's lap:

> Here I am again, crying in the lap of this woman, my mother,
> when I really hate her. She is not a mother. She's awful. I wish
> I could trade her in for another model. I always prostitute my-
> self to her to get Theresa off the hook. (215)

During this marriage therapy session, attempts were made to go back into the formative years of the woman's past to discern whether there are any patterns or events that could account for the difficulties she faces now. When the therapist moves to the present and the marriage difficulty Suzanne is having, he asks her to reenact a moment with her husband that yields a happy memory.

While reenacting a Sunday morning breakfast scene in which husband and wife enjoy the leisurely ritual of eating, the mood changes when her partner says that they will attend a party that evening. Through the reenactment, it becomes evident that her husband is somewhat of a control freak who must be in charge of Suzanne's life. In her desire to please her partner, the therapist concludes that she is reliving moments from her childhood and has not learned how to be independent. The session then leads into Suzanne role-playing a scene with her mother, sister, and husband in which she portrays her autonomy and her newfound assertiveness. Presumably the drama therapy has helped this woman understand an aspect of her life previously not confronted, and as a result, she may be able to build a brighter and better future for herself.

In a drama therapy session, the client comes with an expectation of healing from some physical or psychological scarring. It certainly is not the case in applied theatre that everyone comes with this expectation. While in the applied theatre there is a desire to transform the nature of the world in which we live, teaching artists are not operating from a therapeutic perspective. However, what is interesting about the drama therapist's work is this ability to deal directly with emotional wounds through reenactment. The therapist is not reluctant about releasing emotion, indeed this release seems to be a structural principle.

In the marriage breakdown example here, the therapist believes that committing people directly to an actual situation enables them to perceive something previously hidden about their lives. Through this emotional release comes recognition, which perhaps had not been realized before, of a behavior, an attitude, a way of looking at events. Landy (1986) notes:

> At a time when global peace seems so elusive and when the individual is so often at war with himself, the old solutions— negotiations, medications and modifications—break down. Drama therapy is a new attempt to solve old problems—those of imbalance and protracted threat. (234–35)

A number of pressing ethical questions are raised by drama therapy: What rights do drama therapists have in making connections between past incidents and present dilemmas? How are emotional responses managed by therapists when clients relive shocking personal experiences? When writing about incidents of this nature, do therapists feel bound to ask for clients' permission and approval of written reports? How can drama therapists be certain that their clients will be more empowered as a result of reliving past horrors?

But, more interesting, especially for the applied theatre, is how the drama therapist challenges teaching artists to directly confront emotional situations. The therapist seems to be asking applied theatre workers: Why steer away from emotion? Why seek objective, analogous situations as themes to focus on?

Problem Creation or Problem Solving?

As we are beginning to understand, the term *applied theatre* has been gathering increasing momentum as a useful description of theatre work that takes place in nontheatrical surroundings: most typically, prisons, health and therapy settings, community arts centers, museums and art galleries, support service venues, housing and industrial sites. The applied theatre is powered by a desire to transform human activity through the theatrical medium. For the most part, those who experience applied theatre—those who come to the work as spectators or as participants—have no specific background or necessarily any interest in the theatre form. We presume that those working in the village community in the previous hygiene example are not trained theatre educators nor are the survivors of child abuse aficionados of the art form. Applied theatre comes to them as a way to process issues external agents, in dialogue with communities, regard as significant to the ongoing well-being of the participants. This was certainly the case with Suzanne in the marriage therapy session.

Often, these issues are likened to problems, such as AIDS/HIV awareness (McKenna 2001); race prejudice (Schonmann 1996); homophobia (Garcia 2001); teenage pregnancy, drug and alcohol abuse, cultural discrimination (Grady 2000; Winston 2001), that exist in the community. While drama therapists locate problems that exist for individuals, they are clearly applying theatre within therapeutic settings.

In many respects, applied theatre has much in common with the learning through drama (LTD) movement, which promotes structured improvisation in educational settings to facilitate a learning experience among participants. However, there is one important difference between applied theatre and educational drama. Applied theatre usually involves presentational material from teaching artists as a catalyst for inquiry. Also, applied theatre is often seen as problem-posing education, whereas the LTD movement is powered by facilitators' recognition that certain issues or questions should be addressed. In itself, this problem-posing theatre presents ethical challenges.

The problems to be solved tend to be designated by an outside agent who wants to use or apply theatre as an intervention to prevent unacceptable behavior, to heal a hurt, or to problem solve an issue of social and community concern. A critical element in the success of an applied theatre program is that the community defines the territory to be covered from the project's genesis. This can be a difficult challenge, but communities are less likely to be committed to a project if they have no interest in the subject matter being addressed or if they feel an issue was imposed on them. One further difficulty with likening applied theatre to problem solving is that it immediately suggests that theatre is a solution to deep wounds, can solve political injustices, or is an effective treatment for a range of complaints and evils. This fails to capture the various purposes of applied theatre that previous chapters discussed—to open up possibilities; to heighten awareness; to construct the evolving narratives; to raise the problems of the world, if you will, not to solve them.

BUILDING AN ETHICAL FRAMEWORK

The applied theatre teaching artists' mission—to introduce theatre in a range of communities as a kind of problem-posing interventionist—needs to be treated with sensitivity. Interventionists, by their nature, are not part of the community in which the problem has been diagnosed. They are strangers to the community and are invited in as experts, experts with established patterns of working to initiate problem-posing education for participants. This section highlights the potential pitfalls contained within this approach and how building an ethical framework in the applied theatre should promote a more collaborative endeavor.

Imagine a government department charged with housing low-income families, "the agent," has commissioned a team of teaching artists to combat domestic violence, a growing social problem for those living in subsidized housing projects. The housing projects demonstrate the most impoverished living conditions: unemployment is high, single-parent families are the norm, youths roam the streets at night looking for something to occupy their time. The housing projects are annexed from the main township and have a reputation in the wider community as being centers for criminal activity—prostitution, drug abuse, and racial attacks, to name three—being common.

To combat the growing levels of domestic violence, especially among men in their twenties and thirties who subject their partners to frequent verbal and physical abuse, the agent implements a program of community education whereby support services are dedicated to changing community attitudes. The agent is becoming increasingly frustrated that its conventional manner of treating the *problem* of domestic violence, through distribution of pamphlets that list the various institutions where victims, or survivors, of abuse can seek help, does not seem to be having any impact on the violence.

The agent formulates a strategy that places responsibility on community members to directly interrogate issues of concern. The agent believes that change can only occur when community members become actively committed to seeking an improved lifestyle. The housing projects chosen for this strategy have high levels of social problems, including vandalism, drug and alcohol abuse, domestic violence, and many other forms of community distress. The agent seeks out an applied theatre team, a team who lives in a large city a hundred miles away from the site, to assist the department in transforming the neighborhoods with alarming domestic violence incidents into quiet idyllic centers where conventional notions of family can pervade. The agent offers to pay the team a fee if it can design and implement applied theatre to help the community dialogue around the issue of abuse and to feed into a process of transforming community members' attitudes away from violence as a solution to their problems.

Immediately, readers will notice the dilemma this applied theatre team is faced with. The agent has recognized that there is a problem and has invited an outside organization to come into the community to solve it. The team, not being a part of the community, may be at odds with community members because they are seen as visitors who plan to heal epidemic domestic violence. The agent has been interested in participatory forms of theatre for some time, but this interest has not been a conventional part of the department's "tool kit" for community improvement. Furthermore, the agent has heard about Boal, knew about forum theatre, and was excited by the possibilities it presented. There has been no tradition of using applied theatre at the housing projects as part of the agent's community renewal policy. So, the teaching artists are coming in, possibly to be confronted by bemused looks from the residents, with the sole purpose of changing a cultural problem in a way dictated by the agent.

The agent is keen to have innovative applied theatre programs developed for these impoverished housing sites, and hopes that it will place the residents in immediate and powerful situations so that they can problem *solve* domestic violence issues. Through participating in these situations community members will miraculously see that dependence on domestic violence as a way of solving their grievances is wrong. The agent believes that Boal's participatory theatre strategy shares a mission with its own community renewal strategy, both being powered by a desire to effect self-motivated change in the community.

While it is laudable that this agent recognizes the power of theatre to effect change, considerable pressure is placed on the teaching artists to create a participatory theatre program that will achieve the agent's agenda—lower the rate of domestic violence at deprived housing projects. Further, the agent is concerned that the domestic violence applied theatre project be workshopped in a housing project where there is a high incidence of partner bashing, child abuse, and physical and verbal attacks on family members. Incidents of domestic violence were being reported at the selected site at an increasingly alarming rate. The teaching artists were expected to go into a virtual war zone to solve a difficult social issue. In this instance, the agent is basically admitting that earlier funding initiatives have not been successful, so now it is time to try a new tool—applied theatre.

While the circumstances described here are located within a fictitious scenario, I have been involved in creating applied theatre that focused on domestic violence and was to be presented to victims/survivors in communities similar to this one, where domestic violence is on the rise. One report, for instance, states that one in five young people have seen their mother or stepmother physically assaulted at home. Young people in lower socioeconomic households are more likely to witness such violence compared with those from upper socioeconomic groups. "Young people living with their mother and her new partner were more likely to witness such violence living with both parents. Drunkenness was cited as one of the main causes of [the] domestic violence they had seen" (Harris 2001, 3).

In one project I was involved with, the commissioning agent requested that an applied theatre be designed to enable community members from lower socioeconomic housing projects to process some of the issues raised by domestic violence, to interrogate the circumstances that led to it, and to come up with ways the violence might be avoided. It became clear that if this program was to have resonance with the community, it would need to draw on a model that had proved successful in other applied contexts (Taylor 2002a, 2003). I needed to find exemplars of applied theatre praxis in which the teaching artists had codesigned a satisfying educative program in partnership with the community. Although I had difficulty locating applied theatre about domestic violence, I found an excellent model in the formative work of Moisés Kaufman (2001) and the members of Tectonic Theater Project. It was Kaufman's homophobia project that provided the catalyst and insights for the creative design of the following domestic violence project.

◆ DESIGNING A COMPLEX PROJECT: DOMESTIC VIOLENCE

Kaufman (2001) was interested in an issue of pressing social concern, hate crime. Shocked by the events that led to the murder of a twenty-one-year-old gay college student, Matthew Shepard, who was beaten and left to die after being tied to a fence in a Wyoming prairie in 1998, Kaufman and his company, Tectonic Theatre Project, pondered how theatre form might provide insight into this traumatic event (2001):

> The idea for "The Laramie Project" originated in my desire to learn more about why Matthew Shepard was murdered; about what happened that night; about the town of Laramie. The idea of listening to the citizens' talk really interested me. How is Laramie different from the rest of the country and how is it similar? . . . . What can we as theatre artists do as a response to this incident? And, more concretely: Is theatre a medium that

can contribute to the national dialogue on current events? (11–12)

I was fascinated by how the creative impulse for this project grew out of the playwright's interest in how one community could give rise to such a horrible event. Being from New York City, Kaufman was far-removed from the world of Laramie, Wyoming, and its wide-open spaces. Just as with the teaching artists in the previous domestic violence project, there was apparently little Kaufman had in common with the Laramie community, so to discover more about the town he and his theatre company visited it.

Kaufman's play, "The Laramie Project," is based on interviews conducted with Laramie residents. It would be these interviews, the words of community members and those of the interviewers, that would be scripted into the play: "Little did we know that we would devote two years of our lives to this project . . . and [have] conducted over two hundred interviews" (2001, 12). Kaufman was interested in how he could use these interviews as the basis for a dramatic work; it would be the community members themselves who would help sculpt a dramatic product.

Rather than present a dramatization of the events surrounding Shepard's death, Kaufman selected a documentary theatre style, sometimes referred to as *theatrical* or *verbatim reportage*—the actors recreate snatches of the interviews conducted (Albert 2001). We never actually meet Shepard in the play; his life is created through the recollections and observations of others. By not presenting Shepard, the playwright is able to provide accounts of his life from multiple perspectives. Audience members are then challenged to create their own perspective of him. This technique struck me as richly resonant for constructing the domestic violence project.

"The Laramie Project" has been presented in a variety of venues, including schools, and is currently experiencing a renaissance, partly because Shepard's death is representative of a range of hate crimes. Presenting the play enables communities to come together to discuss tolerance and diversity: "And much of what the play has to convey as a teaching tool is embedded not just in its content but in its form. No one portrays one character alone; everyone has to represent multiple, sometimes opposing characters" (Shewey 2002,

7). This play also works as a teaching tool because audiences can commit to the situation rather than to a character.

Similarly, in the applied theatre, we aim to have participants play numerous roles so that they can begin to witness the variety of perspectives that power any given situation (Shewey 2002):

> "The Laramie Project" is ultimately a meeting between two communities: a community of speakers (the residents of Laramie) and a community of listeners (the Tectonic Theatre members who interviewed them). As a theatre event, it serves as a model for a way of speaking tough truths and listening respectfully—a form of communication that human beings crave but that is rarely experienced these days anywhere in public, especially in the news media, where sound bites pass for insight and competing monologues masquerade as debate. (7)

Given that the teaching artists in the domestic violence project had no experience of life at the deprived rural housing projects, an extended field trip would be necessary to gather and analyze data that could tell us something about the communities' experience, especially around the topic of domestic violence. Interviews can be a rich source of data when designing applied theatre projects; when speaking to a wide range of community members, teaching artists begin to get a sense of what it means to live within the community where the project is to be presented. The data yielded can often be quite challenging especially when stereotypical attitudes are emerging.

Just as Kaufman came across the bigots and the homophobes, the domestic violence project demonstrates a range of prejudicial attitudes toward the roles of men and women. These attitudes can be confronting to teaching artists who sometimes believe they have far more enlightened or worldly views of a given situation than those of their interviewees. It is crucial for teaching artists to take a nonjudgmental stance and allow their interviewees to speak freely and honestly. Once data has been collected, we begin a process of analyzing the themes as they relate to domestic violence and then construct a program, being sure not identify any of our informants.

Staging a Discussion

The site visit demonstrated that there were high levels of vandalism within certain sections of the township. Nuisance and annoyance issues were common, with numerous complaints to police about late-night parties, drug scenes on the streets, and/or aggressive behavior from young people. There were no dividing fences between neighbors' properties which meant that often one would see young people using both front yards and backyards as thoroughfares, causing aggravation within the township. The unemployment rate in the town was high, and there was a concentration of public (subsidized) housing in the projects. Domestic violence seemed to be a huge problem, with many we spoke to describing it as significant within the community.

Interviews with the residents were conducted on a range of topics, including violence in the community. Alienation became a significant theme. After returning from the field site, we decided to create as incomplete a text as we possibly could. This incompleteness would permit participants to project their own stories or versions of the events. In projects like these, it is important that teaching artists do not propose their own solutions. Given the lack of sustained involvement the artists had in the community, these would hardly be credible anyway. We were not experts on domestic violence; no one in our group had had direct experience with domestic violence, or they did not admit to such. So the stories of domestic violence told us would be caught within the dramatic episodes we would create.

Guiding Questions
- *What constitutes a domestic violence incident?*
- *How should domestic violence incidents be handled in the community?*
- *What are the responsibilities of community members when they are faced with knowledge about domestic violence?*

The teaching artists constructed the following scenario.

Scenario
The participants (audience members) meet Brenda, the town gossip. She speaks about her life at one of the houses in the project. She comments on the different racial groups, the street kids, the police presence or lack of presence. She seems a caricature, but nonetheless speaks truth through her naïveté. She tells of the drugs, the alcohol abuse, the lack of money to pay rent, the problems

with the housing agents who keep asking for improvements. She hates the fact that her house has no fence because local children keep running through her yard. She mentions the neighbors who moved in a month ago. "Something funny is going on there," she says. "The man comes home late. The blinds are shut." We next meet Brenda's neighbors. The tempo changes as we witness an aggressive man who controls his "woman." In a stylized presentation, the participants witness what seems a potentially alarming incident of domestic violence.

Participation

The audience first hotseat Brenda and are provided with opportunities to question her about her life in the project. The facilitator asks whether they, the participants, know people like Brenda. How would they describe her life? Does she speak of truth within their region? Following the man/woman presentation, the participants are asked whether this woman has any other options besides staying with the man. The options are canvassed and one is selected. For instance, if the participants believed the woman could go to speak with a counselor, they become the counselor and offer advice to the woman. The appropriateness of that advice is then investigated. The applied theatre concludes with a discussion about whether people like the woman and the man exist here and what the community's responsibilities are when it knows of incidents of domestic violence. A social worker from a government agency speaks to participants about available services.

Comment

This program requires four teaching artists: facilitator, Brenda, man, woman; it was to be presented during "Domestic Violence Week" in a community center at one of the housing projects in the township. The function of Brenda, as the opening presentation, was more for light-hearted relief because participants knew this project was to focus on domestic violence, and, more than likely, everyone had their own expectations as to what was to occur. In all probability, participants would have expected that they were going to be preached at because this event was hosted by the township's housing office.

Topics like domestic violence need to be handled delicately and we were determined to include someone from the local counseling service who had experience with this issue in our presentation. This person prepared an information booklet on domestic violence and was prepared to speak at the program's closure about what services would be available. Brenda is clearly a comic creation; she is the busybody who seems to have gossip about the entire town readily at hand.

The scene between the man and the woman is where the heart of this project lay; it was devised based on interview data that had been collected. The man and woman are not an actual couple living in the township but are representatives of the kind of relationship which sometimes harbors domestic violence. This relationship was scripted following the teaching artists' analysis of the data collected. The encounter between the man and the woman became the catalyst for the participatory theatre that emerged. The following text is a sample of the dialogue that occurred between them. Two actors face each other, standing some distance apart. They are anonymously named *Man* and *Woman:*

WOMAN: I live in Yalumba *(Yalumba is a fictitious name)*. I like gardening and watching TV. Sometimes I go window shopping in town.

MAN *(Steps in):* I live in Yalumba. I love payday. I really love going to the bars with me buddies. Sometimes I do work on the projects for money.

WOMAN *(Steps in):* I live up here. There isn't much to do. I have to keep the house clean.

MAN *(Steps in):* I live up here. Nothing really happens. I go out with me buddies.

WOMAN *(Steps in):* Up here. Kids rule the streets. He spends time with his buddies at the bars. I don't have many buddies.

MAN *(Steps in):* Up here. Some people are scared to go out on the streets by themselves. I'm not.

WOMAN *(Steps in):* In here. He comes home from the bar, after seeing his buddies. I don't go out much.

MAN *(Steps in):* In here. I come home from the bar and watch TV. I always have control of the remote.

WOMAN (*Steps in*): Out there. I'm sure they hear when he comes
   home from the bar. But no one says anything.
MAN (*Steps in*): Out there. I don't have as much power as I do in
   here. (*Raises hand to woman's face*)
MAN: I don't go out much. (*Turns head as he goes to hit her*)[1]

The words in this scenario are loaded with the questions the
housing agent requested us to process: What constitutes a domestic violence incident? How can we problem-pose issues of domestic violence? How can incidents of domestic violence be overcome?
The text demonstrates a power relationship where Man uses his
physicality to wield control over Woman. Her oppression in the
household is apparent. She seems to allow the dominance of Man
to continue. The words are so simple, "I don't go out much," but
they contain information about a genuine dilemma Woman is in.
It seems that she has no alternatives, that she feels she cannot get
out of this relationship. Perhaps she loves Man despite the fact
that he abuses her. Our research indicates that many victims of
domestic violence have great love for their partners and have
developed a codependency. Man is not presented sympatheti-
cally; he treats Woman as just another chattel, like a TV remote
control.

After the presentation of this scenario, the audience—in this
instance members of the community where incidents of domestic
violence have occurred—were asked to participate in a number of
encounters in order to process the issues raised. Because we were
dealing with potential victims of domestic violence, and with participants who were inexperienced in drama activity, it was crucial
for the applied theatre work to evolve in a nonthreatening manner. It was critical for participants to feel empowered to speak up.
Once the scene was presented, facilitators probed for participants'
responses to the material. A number of closed/open questions
helped us explore the Man/Woman scenario.

Facilitator: How long has Woman been living in Yalumba?
   Are these two married? How long?
   Does Woman think this situation is normal?

---

[1]My thanks to Beth King for her work on the domestic violence project.

How long has it been going on?
What options does Woman have?
How might she remove herself from this situation?
Who might she go and talk to for help?

Using this line of questioning, an identity for Woman can slowly emerge. Participants begin to project their own reading of Woman's life and a composite character is made. The final question about the options Woman has and who she might talk to launches a process whereby participants can enter a scene and give advice to Woman. The group might decide that Woman should speak to a social worker, or to a friend, family member, neighbor. The facilitator selects one of these and invites the group to represent that social worker, or that friend or neighbor. The teaching artist playing Woman does not make it easy for participants to help her. The teaching artist has difficulty with the advice; she is uncertain about how to proceed, she asks participants to demonstrate ways of overcoming the problematic situations she finds herself in.

Facilitator (*to participants*)**:** When Woman comes in, I want you to draw out of her what is happening, talk to her, make her figure out that she might make her life circumstances better. You can help her. She might not be willing to hear your advice.

Enter Woman. She is hotseated. Woman is troubled, noncommunicative. She says things like, "I love my partner," "I don't know if I can leave him," "Where am I going to go?" As readers can deduce, the emphasis here is on the participants' voicing of possibilities for Woman to consider. The teaching artist playing Woman, while not wanting to block, works to create disruptive or confusing moments. The applied theatre program aims to open up dialogue; it invites participants to listen to, and to confront, immediate dilemmas that exist within their communities.

At the close of this particular program, participants consider whether Woman strikes them as an authentic victim of domestic violence. When there is some disagreement, members of the group are asked to enact their own version of Woman, and the participants assume roles such as social worker or neighbor, that they have committed to in the previous episode.

In this work, we are clearly drawing on the praxis of Boal (2001) and others interested in applied theatre as a vehicle for transformation. The objective is to enable participants to apply the art form as a means for resolving issues the program is investigating. Again it is community members who power the evolution of the piece at every phase. It is their words and experiences that are represented in the applied theatre.

CONCLUDING STATEMENTS ABOUT ETHICS

I am indebted to James Thompson (2000) and his work about prison theatre for helping me understand that often a central principle in applied theatre is its break with certainty, that rather than pushing a moral platitude or a statement of political correctness, the applied theatre practitioner is working toward ambiguous and incomplete moments. As Thompson writes:

> If theatre was only a skills training method for probation clients to practice roles that they could then perform in later life, we [potentially lose] the complexity of the theatre workshop and performance process as a dynamic, difficult, rich moment in itself. (4)

When drawing so strongly on participants' words and gestures in the creation of the domestic violence project, it is inevitable that complexity in human relations will be demonstrated. The domestic violence project aimed to highlight that complexity by structuring a dynamic scenario, which suggested that there is no simple solution to resolving difficult and challenging situations. We agree with Kaufman's claim that such snapshots of human endeavor push "the boundaries" of what theatre can do. The interviews with community residents, and the applied theatre that emerged, shared the desire of "The Laramie's Project" to permit "the community to talk about their feelings," to raise their ideals and desires (Albert 2001, R19).

The evaluation of this work has been written about elsewhere (Taylor 2002b), but what became apparent as the teaching artists conducted follow-up interviews with the commissioning agent, residents, participants, and observers of the program were the diverse perspectives around the project. It is inevitable that applied theatre artists who come into communities like these are going to stand out as strangers. Isolated communities are not necessarily familiar with or supportive of the purposes of an applied theatre. Just as Kaufman found that residents of Laramie were "initially sus-picious" of Tectonic's presence in the community (Albert 2001, R19), I wondered how community members would respond to our presence. Is it ethical for teaching artists to enter communities with the intention of opening up dialogue on complex and chal-lenging issues, especially when they have no direct experience with the issues? Is it possible for one applied theatre project to produce anything but a cursory exploration of an issue? While applied the-atre teaching artists can begin to generate a conversation about domestic violence, is it really their right and responsibility to do this? And, what kind of follow-up work is needed?

A one-time domestic violence presentation, in which partici-pants encounter a fictitious domestic violence program powered by real-life experiences, is not an ongoing process that fully delves into the underlying causes of the violence. In some rural commu-nities like the previously described fictitious site, where resources are few and far between and where there may be a desperate short-age of family income and social services, the cause of domestic vio-lence might very well lie outside the home and be generated by institutional and societal factors. For instance, if the housing of-fice responsible for maintaining the estates does not provide peo-ple adequate privacy and protection through the construction of fences, there is an inevitable sense of vulnerability. If jobs don't exist, a partner's unemployment could generate a huge domestic strain.

Applied theatre workers cannot be conned into thinking that they are the saviors of the community. It seems clear that the issue of sustainable change in people's lives is not going to be adequately addressed through isolated applied theatre demonstrations. Cer-tainly, applied theatre can help facilitate discussion, look at why incidents like domestic violence might occur, and pose some temporary possibilities for what people in these situations might do. But, to have a larger impact it seems that a more sustained com-munity commitment would be required. Further, applied theatre should be seen as a part of a wider assignment and activity by the agents who commission such programs. Agents should not divest themselves of their responsibility for social concern issues. They should be working in partnership with the applied theatre, and if they aren't, the teaching artists should find strategies to include the agent in the project's design and implementation.

It is very difficult to know what kind of impact the applied theatre program is having on people's lives.

How do applied theatre artists document a sustained change in people's lives?

Should applied theatre workers even be interested in documenting such change?

Is it ethical for applied theatre workers to begin to construe their mission as one of creating social change?

What moral authority do applied theatre artists share other than a commitment to theatre as an aesthetic medium to help participants act, reflect, and transform?

It is clear from the examples in this text, nevertheless, that applied theatre can play a role in helping community members dialogue about the kind of lives they lead and the futures they would like to create. Although it might be ethically wrong for applied theatre workers to promulgate moral behaviors, they are certainly well armed to create situations in which people can have conversations about what is or is not possible. The trick, it seems to me, is to set up work that holds strong resonances for participants to project their own readings and their own lives into the scenarios being presented. The days of fashioning cleverly constructed well-made plays in which dilemmas are happily resolved, conflicts are cleared, and lives are reborn, perhaps, send out the wrong messages. The reality is that life is complex, people can be inconsistent and their actions contradictory. A quick read of the daily newspapers reveals that inequities occur wherever we look. The applied theatre worker needs to be conscious of these realities and be aware of their abilities to effect change. Is it ethical for participants to believe that they have access to resources when, in fact, they don't?

In the depiction of the domestic violence project here, applied theatre becomes an aesthetic medium to probe pressing societal, moral, and political concerns. The applied theatre is not simply theatre employed as a teaching tool in educational settings, but it can move into a variety of community and vocational settings where the participants may have little or no interest in conventional theatre. The participants' interest is driven by what the theatre work says to them about life's challenges and how they can apply the theatre form as a transformative vehicle for investigating such challenges.

I agree with the sentiments of Ackroyd (2000) who argues that two of the central characteristics of applied theatre are an intention (1) to generate change, and (2) to have audience members participate. A further characteristic, one might argue, is the artfulness of the theatre form that leads to such change and participation. This chapter documents how we need to be sensitive to the ethical imperatives applied theatre workers experience and reveals some of the challenges in designing work that can be powered by human endeavor. We have seen how applied theatre aims to capture participants within the art form. The applied theatre, then, is not always powered by a didactic, or agit-prop, orientation, which often instructs or shocks, but by a desire to allow the theatre form to be an instrument to provoke transformation and participation.

Programs in applied theatre have now been established at the Universities of Exeter and Manchester (UK), Griffith University (Australia), and New York University, where students can gain applied theatre undergraduate and postgraduate degrees. There is also a new journal dedicated to applied theatre research—*Applied Theatre Researcher* (www.gu.edu.au/centre/atr). As well, we are noticing how the TfD movement has a strong link to the global aims of applied theatre (Odhiambo 2001; Van Erven 2001).

Although, clearly, a lot more work needs to be done in researching the efficacy of the term *applied theatre*, there is compelling evidence that many have found it useful (O'Connor 2001). It is my hope that this chapter will prompt a further conversation about different applied theatre projects and the ethical challenges field workers experience as they construct programs.

5

EVALUATING APPLIED THEATRE

We are now faced with the challenge of how to evaluate applied theatre programs. What criteria should we draw on as we begin a conversation about the effectiveness of applied theatre? Who benefits from an evaluation? To what extent does evaluation help improve the quality of the applied theatre? What are the most appropriate techniques for discerning information about progress and achievement? These questions are complex ones and not easily examined. There are those who would argue that evaluation is too hard-edged and only suits the purposes of the external agents who commission applied theatre. Others would say that evaluation is necessary to ensure the ongoing maturity and survival of the applied theatre.

If applied theatre workers are not constantly examining their praxis, there is little indication that they are scrutinizing the impact they are having in the field. I am interested in how reflective applied theatre teaching artists are. Reflection is critical because it demonstrates that applied theatre workers are asking what is happening at any given point as they implement the work. Good applied theatre teaching artists are able to constantly reflect and evaluate how participants are engaging with their programs; reflection also helps with the monitoring of how teaching artists are interacting.

Reflection, a recursive process, does not happen merely at the end of the event, after the teaching artists have returned from the field. It is consistent and sustained reflection that helps shape the quality of applied theatre, especially when the work has significant emotional impact. How do we create applied theatre that is necessary? That can change people's lives? How do we ensure that the applied theatre engages its participants? That it releases them into new ways of seeing, hearing, and thinking? How can we be sure that applied theatre has achieved its stated objectives? Evaluation has a role to play here.

I am interested in evaluation reports that highlight the recursive, reflective thinking of those who participate in applied theatre, not in evaluation reports written solely by external agents who have little to do with the process of creating the applied theatre. If evaluation is to have any real purpose in applied theatre, teaching artists themselves need to be involved in reflective thinking. Of course, they can be helped in this process by an external agent; but unless there is a grounded attempt to critically appraise the applied theatre by those responsible for implementing the program, evaluation only serves the needs of the bureaucrats and the funders.

It is unlikely that applied theatre teaching artists will grow until they scrutinize their work and ask themselves some key questions:

- *How do I know if the applied theatre was successful?*
- *What do the varying constituents involved with the applied theatre have to say about the work's effectiveness?*
- *How do I go about determining progress and achievement?*

For these reasons, there is a great deal that applied theatre workers can learn from the interpretive-research movement, which privileges the ideas, attitudes, and desires of those within the creative moment. There needs to be a more holistic evaluation in which teaching artists see themselves as implicated in the effectiveness of applied theatre. When teaching artists liken their work to that of the reflective practitioner, they will ensure the production of credible evaluation reports that include the voices of the various stakeholders who have an investment in the program's success.

WHY EVALUATE?

Evaluation refers to the search for information that indicates effectiveness, which can mean a variety of different things based on who actually wants the evaluation, of a given phenomena. To the applied theatre teaching artist, effectiveness might not mean the same as it does to the commissioning agent. Commissioning agents may not be interested in reading long, detailed case studies about participants' growth in understanding; they might want to read statistical information about how the applied theatre improved behavior or transformed attitudes. Such information can be very difficult to attain, especially in remote communities where there might not be time to interview or survey participants about what they gained from the material. Nevertheless, knowing who it is for is central to how to conduct the evaluation.

While evaluation can occur at any given point in time within a program, it is usually a product that occurs at or toward the end of the event. I would like to challenge this notion that evaluation is an end-on measure. Although evaluation usually has a summative quality to it, applied theatre workers need to constantly appraise whether they are achieving the aims and objectives they have outlined. Although evaluation reports can make generalizations, or global statements, about how well a program was presented and how well it was received by all the main constituents, evaluations should also include information about how the various interest groups responded at any given moment during the project's design and implementation. As programs are being devised, this information can be invaluable to the applied theatre worker.

The realities are that evaluation serves a number of different purposes and when these purposes are confused, some difficulties for the funders, teaching artists, participants, and various vested interests that accompany the applied theatre can emerge. An example of this confusion became apparent recently when I found out that a program's funder was disappointed with the completed written evaluation of the theatre project. The funder had been anticipating that the applied theatre evaluation would yield statistical data that would demonstrate the theatre's effectiveness in altering people's attitudes and/or changing their behaviors. Because this data was not forthcoming in the evaluation, the funder lodged an official complaint and threatened legal action.

Those who commission applied theatre are often intent on receiving reports they can use to ensure sustained funding. They can be less than supportive of reports that are critical of the program or point to weaknesses in it. For instance, it is not uncommon for artist-in-residency programs to commission reports on the agency's effectiveness by companies that specialize in evaluation. Because these companies are being paid by the arts agency, there can be subtle pressure on them to provide laudatory or highly supportive reports of the agency's work. These evaluation reports can be crucial to the agency's survival and can be used as evidence in applications that seek further financial support.

If the evaluation is meant directly for the commissioning agent who can use the report to sell the work to others and to secure additional funding, then those who write the reports might need to be sensitive to the audience. If, on the other hand, the evaluation is for the teaching artists so that they can solicit knowledge about what was successful in their planning, and what wasn't, the report has more of a pragmatic benefit; the applied theatre team can then use the data to help them in future design and implementation. I believe that the beneficiaries of the evaluation should be the teaching artists, participants, and the wider applied theatre community. It is imperative that evaluations feed into long-term strategic planning and not merely document what commissioning agents want to hear.

The best forms of evaluation determine effectiveness using a range of techniques to gather data from multiple perspectives: qualitative and quantitative. *Quantitative* refers to evidence that can be easily collected and analyzed; usually this information requires simple and short responses that can be readily tabulated. An example of this approach is a proforma—usually a series of propositions to agree/not agree with—for participants to complete.

Check the statements you agree with:

☐ *I enjoyed this presentation.*
☐ *I learned a lot about the issue being presented.*
☐ *I had not considered the suggestions for overcoming the issues the program presented.*

Proformas might include multiple-choice questions, which limit the responses participants can provide. In the domestic violence program, one could survey participants' reactions to the following.

What advice would you give Woman in the program? (Check one box only)

☐ *Leave Man*
☐ *Stand up for herself*

☐ *Seek advice from the local counseling agency*
☐ *Move in with a friend*
☐ *Other: Please state* _____

A difficulty with seeking information that limits the responses of participants in this way is that it will not provide the kind of penetrating and reflective accounts of what understandings were being generated from the program. While it is helpful to prepare surveys and questionnaires, the participants in the applied theatre might not have the time or interest in completing them. It can be very difficult to survey audiences in community settings where there are transient populations. However, external agents who commission applied theatre may be more interested in the generalizations drawn from these checklists because they can be read quickly and easily communicated to a range of audiences.

I am more interested in the evidence to be gained from qualitative reports. *Qualitative* reports are about formulating in-depth understandings of the perspectives of the stakeholders who come to applied theatre. The qualitative report embarks on a comprehensive inquiry of the multiple and shifting perspectives surrounding an applied theatre event. These perspectives can sometimes contradict one another and when this happens the qualitative inquirer needs to be able to probe further and attempt to account for the diverse and contradictory ideas.

I would now like to move on to how qualitative reports, which highlight the reflective praxis of those who come to the applied theatre, are especially revealing. I am advocating here a form of inquiry known as *reflective praxis*—teaching artists, with their constituents, work together to yield knowledge that is critical to the future of the applied theatre.

SEARCHING FOR EVIDENCE

The best evaluations, in my mind, are those that endeavor to get at what really occurred in the field setting and whether what happened was rewarding or important to all of the stakeholders. These evaluations attempt to include numerous perspectives about the event, including those of teaching artists, participants, and a range of interest groups who have a stake in the project. Poor evaluations are those in which the conclusions drawn are based on a lack of substantive and informative data. These evaluations often present findings based on scant or piecemeal evidence or evidence that has been collected from only a select number of perspectives. The challenge is to find those data-collection and analysis strategies that will provide logical and coherent responses to the work.

When formulating criteria for which applied theatre should be evaluated, we must remind ourselves of what the projects aim to achieve. In this book, readers will have observed how applied theatre is driven by guiding questions such as the following:

- *How might applied theatre help survivors and victims process a painful past and build a hopeful future?*
- *What applied theatre strategies will enable participants to investigate the issues being explored?*
- *How might teaching artists implicate participants in a dilemma that should be interrogated?*
- *To what extent can the applied theatre empower communities to effect change in their neighborhoods?*

The aims of the applied theatre, expressed as questions, should be at the forefront of an evaluation. Remember applied theatre does not aim to present simple solutions to complex problems. What it does hope to achieve is to enable participants to become more reflective about a given issue and to highlight how they might begin a dialogue around the issue.

It can be difficult to generate good data on applied theatre events because the programs are ephemeral, transitory, and occur in relatively short periods of time. Nevertheless, it seems to me that there is a pressing need to solicit appropriate and manageable information that will feed directly into the planning, implementation, and evaluation of future applied theatre programs. We must be careful, however, that we don't make evaluation more important than the experience itself. Nothing can be more deadly to the applied theatre than those teaching artists who give out questionnaires at the beginning of the presentation. It would be far preferable to invite participants to stay late to discuss whether they believe the program met its aims.

We must not forget that applied theatre is a human-centered event powered by a variety of agendas, interests, and expectations.

Just as Kaufman found when he was collecting data for "The Laramie Project," communities are driven by multiple and transforming perspectives. His text attempts to incorporate a range of opinions about the horrible murder of Matthew Shepard and its impact on the Laramie community as well as on the artists charged with the responsibility of rendering the Shepard story into a theatrical event. Applied theatre should be powered equally by acknowledging different perspectives in its attempt to seek justice and equity.

As I write these words, I contemplate the desperately confusing times we live in. Every day seems to bring a continual parade of government inquiries into misdemeanors and fraud. Every day provides a record of leaders who deliberately mislead and undermine the public. I am reminded of the frequent abuses of power and privilege that can have responsible citizens physically and sexually harass those they employ. While I watch warmongering images, hear more about the politics of hate, view stories on ethnic-cleansing, learn again about weapons of mass destruction, new crusades, and terrorists' desire for revenge and worldwide catastrophe, I can only be reminded that there is no one singular version of truth. There are those who would have us believe that there is a singularity—a mainstream uniformity, which will provide comfort and solace. But as yet another teenager goes armed into a classroom murdering his classmates, as we hear of sniper attacks with no rhyme or reason, and as we witness the bludgeoning of parents by young children, I cannot be comforted by the notion of a singular truth. Indeed, it would be dangerous if I were comforted by such a notion.

Evaluation reports that aim to present such a unitary version of a complex whole far underestimate the power of applied theatre to present wide-ranging and inclusive viewpoints. As I go into communities where poverty is around each street corner, where racial groups struggle to speak let alone be heard, where guns are freely available, where school kids are hungry and go to school to be fed, and then contrast these states with affluent neighborhoods where residents make sure the homeless are never seen on the streets, I am reminded of the great divide that still exists. Applied theatre has a role to play in presenting such extremes and in promoting rich conversations around them.

An evaluation report that wants to deny such complexity fails to acknowledge why applied theatre exists. Evaluations should aim to get at the shades of grey and air divergent viewpoints. There are those who might argue that evidence does exist to support one proposition and that there are no exceptions to the rule—in other words, that one cause leads to one effect. Rarely do applied theatre participants act with a homogeneous viewpoint; there are always differences of opinions and varied suggestions for trying alternate strategies. Evaluation reports need to account for the negative cases, those examples that are not like-minded, those that don't necessarily fit into the mainstream.

While some evaluators would have us believe that there is *a truth*, my experience tells me otherwise. Truths are constructed from within the circumstances that people find themselves in, and just as those circumstances may change at any given time, so might the truths. There was a time when evaluators were pressured to establish clinical experiments when gathering data. Question-naires would be completed, confidentiality would be preserved, multiple-choice questions would be fed into machines to produce neat statistical charts. These charts would, it seems, evidence a truth. Some evaluators would establish an experimental study with two groups—control and treatment. The control group would not participate in the activity under investigation but the treatment group would. Both groups would have the same test at the beginning and at the end of the experiment, usually a written test, and the results would be graded and tabulated. Clearly this form of controlling the data is not possible in the applied theatre. Written data-collection forms are not always the most revealing and can limit the quality of the responses provided.

Evaluators need to appreciate that there is more than one way to gather evidence. Reports that attempt to describe rather than measure learning processes may be far more illuminating. Evaluations that draw on the long-established tradition of qualitative inquiry in education, social sciences, and the humanities might help us get to the complexities of applied theatre.

Reports that demonstrate how the applied theatre promotes the ongoing reflexive praxis of the teaching artists, the participants, and all others who come to the event might be more helpful to the future planning of applied theatre. I am interested in evaluations that will be beneficial to those who come to the applied theatre— reports that actually can feed into the development of the work.

BECOMING MORE REFLECTIVE

The applied theatre is a reflective theatre in which people encounter worlds in a state of flux. It is incumbent on applied theatre to challenge participants to interrogate these worlds, to reflect on them, to transform them. Evaluations of applied theatre should be descriptive accounts to promote further conversations about the work, its merits, and how it did or did not achieve its objectives. Evaluation reports should endeavor to help in the reflexive praxis of those who make, present, reflect, and support applied theatre.

For some time now, I have been interested in the notion of the reflective practitioner and the circumstances in which people become more conscious of how they are having an impact on their world. When applied theatre is operating at its most effective, the teaching artists, the participants, the funders, and all those connected to it become reflective practitioners. So, who are the reflective practitioners, and how can this stance access the multiplicity of visions and permit the multiplicity of truths I am interested in?

When people hear the term *reflective practitioner*, they often think of intense, introspective activity, or navel gazing—a more inward-thinking approach to evaluation. While I would agree that the stance of the reflective practitioner requires the ability to scrutinize the immediate context, there is the unfortunate connotation that navel gazing implies being lost in oneself, or removed from the group. I don't see myself as a navel gazer. On the contrary, the reflective practitioner stance demands a discovery of self, a recognition of how one interacts with others, and how others read and are read by this interaction. It is a stance peculiarly neglected in the applied theatre, perhaps because of various misconceptions and concerns about how the stance interacts with sustained inquiry, or perhaps because of the dedication that it involves. However, it is a central argument in this chapter that for evaluators to ignore the merits of the reflective practitioner design they need to remain ignorant to the kind of artistic processes that are the lifeblood of applied theatre.

The work of Chris Argyris and Donald Schön (1974) at the Massachusetts Institute of Technology has been invaluable in my understanding of the reflective practitioner, especially due to their recognition that professional competence is linked to an ability to try out ideas "on-line" and to understand how these trials might lead to improvement within the workplace context. In his 1983 book, *The Reflective Practitioner*, Schön examines five professions—engineering, architecture, management, psychotherapy, and town planning—to show how professionals go about solving the questions, dilemmas, and problems they encounter on a daily basis. Although he does not specifically examine applied theatre, Schön emphasizes artistic processes, notably improvisational modes of inquiry, as being vital to the ongoing and sustained competence of professional development. Evaluation that does not take into account the reflective practice of the individuals under study can be incomplete.

In brief, Schön claims that the bureaucrats' and the technicians' language, which is housed in the positivist and neopositivist world of technical rationality, is not immediately translatable into daily practice situations. When dealing with the immediate challenges professionals encounter, they not only draw on an intuitive knowledge base as a way for dealing with this challenge—what Schön refers to as knowing-in-action—but on their ability to reflect-in-action as a means for directing their own and others' behavior. This immediate process of reflection is characterized by a complex internal dialogue, which requires prompt decisions about what the practitioner is observing and how those observations should influence behavior; according to Schön (1983):

> When someone reflects-in-action, he [sic] becomes a researcher in the practice context. He is not dependent on the categories of established theory and technique, but constructs a new theory of the unique case. His inquiry is not limited to a deliberation about means which depends on a prior agreement about ends. He does not keep means and ends separate, but defines them interactively as he frames a problematic situation. He does not separate thinking from doing, ratiocinating his way to a decision

which he must later convert to action. Because his experimenting is a kind of action, implementation is built into his inquiry. This reflection-in-action can proceed, even in situations of uncertainty or uniqueness, because it is not bound by the dichotomies of Technical Rationality. (68–69)

In evaluation reports, we should include accounts of how the applied theatre is operating as a reflective event. Rather than pursuing other people's ideas of truth, reflective practitioners interrogate the character of their own truths. In applied theatre, we want participants to confront their values, their prejudices, and their notions of the good and the bad. We want to specifically establish work that challenges participants to look at themselves in new ways. Because this interrogation is happening-in-action throughout the project, evaluation reports need to look at the kind of stances participants adopted during the work.

Although there are aspects of Schön's model that do not translate easily into applied theatre; for instance, his weighted emphasis on problem solving and experimental inquiry tend to defy the interpretive features of the paradigm often required in applied theatre, Schön's text does highlight one of the principal means through which the applied theatre operates, that is, through reflection-in-action, or a reflective conversation with the situation (268). Evaluation reports should attempt to track the reflective conversations that participants and teaching artists are having during the applied theatre.

I am drawing an important distinction here between reflection-*in*-action and reflection-*on*-action. Readers probably are familiar with the kind of action research models, or the approaches to teacher research, inspired by Lawrence Stenhouse (1975) in England. These models have been quite popular in educational research given that they empower teachers to take control of their own work. However, it is important to note that there is a significant difference between the action research model and that informed by reflective practice. Whereas action researchers tend to emphasize the result rather than the process as a culminating activity (i.e., one plans, one acts, one reflects, then one plans again), reflective practitioner researchers are concerned with documenting and understanding the tacit and known knowledge base that enables reflection-in-action to occur. The following are the kinds of questions reflective practitioners ask:

- Why do applied theatre participants respond in the way they do?
- What leads teaching artists to make on-the-spot changes in the applied theatre?
- How do participants work their way out of the dilemmas presented to them?
- What course of action do facilitators assume when they meet challenging interventions from their participants?
- How do funders' needs impact on the applied theatre?
- How can teaching artists respond in the here and now?

For applied theatre evaluators, there is an attractiveness to the reflective practitioner design because it honors intuitive and emergent processes that inform the aesthetic event. At the heart of applied theatre is a willingness by both teaching artists and participants to transcend the boundaries of fixed realities and to enter virtual ones. I would argue that the ability to transcend and to enter occurs in part because they engage immediately with the situation and allow that situation to work on them.

The opening of Stephen Sondheim's musical, "Sunday in the Park with George," is a classic illustration of the decisive features of reflective practice and suggests those qualities toward which applied theatre should aim. As the curtain rises on a stark white space, the audience is greeted by the nineteenth-century French neoimpressionist Georges Seurat. As this figure sits downstage with canvases and easels in front of him, a series of ascending arpeggios press the artist into motion. While playfully manipulating the tools of his craft, he verbalizes his understanding of significant form (Sondheim & Lapine [1984] 1991):

White: A blank page or canvas
The challenge: bring order to the whole.
Through design.
Composition.
Tension.
Balance.

Light.
And harmony. (17–18)

The images he dabs and daubs begin to inhabit the world of the stage. Just as Seurat's white canvas is transformed into blocks of colored patterns, the theatrical work is swept into motion. The artist's reflective conversation with himself, with the artwork, with the people and objects that inhabit the work, and with the audience is what gives the craft its life. The artist's reflection-in-action brings the virtual world into being.

I am aware that this being is not powered simply by the creative energy that inhabits the making phases of artistic endeavor. Artworks are constructed through intense phases of reflection after an activity as well, and I do not want to be setting up oppositional modes of reflective activity. However, contained within the history of artworks, especially in the applied performing arts, is a recognition that their power rests on lived experience.

Many American dancers of Martha Graham's era, for instance, resisted and scorned the celluloid image, valuing the impression that a single performance would leave on the audience. Graham's dances were a reflection-in-action; they achieved the features of Schön's on-line exploration—a willingness to draw on and submit to one's breadth of worldly experiences when bringing form to an idea. "Life today is nervous, sharp and zig-zag," Graham once said. "It often stops in mid air. . . . It is what I want for my dances" (Gardner 1993, 274).

While years of technique went into Graham's dances, the aesthetic experience for the audience was generated not only by skill but also by her structured spontaneity. Both dancer and spectator engage with or submit to the artwork at the moment in which it is realized in form. For Graham and many other artists, reflection not only happens before and after the performed event, but informs the very event itself. Applied theatre too is powered by a reflection-in-action—ideas are rethought in process and techniques are refined or dropped based on how participants engage with them.

Little is known about the character of reflection-in-action. Most of us rarely have time to examine what factors lead to competence because we are too intent on trying to implement, or evaluate, others' versions of competence. Rarely do we see ourselves as the experts, as the ones who can know and reflect-in-action; yet without immediate and ongoing reflective activity, it is difficult to see how applied theatre would ever occur.

We are constantly confounded by notions of singular truth and authoritative ways of going about our work. Perhaps artists like Graham contribute to this confusion, given their emphasis on a firm skill base and a grounding in the content bases of the discipline. "The body must be tempered by hard, definite technique— the science of dance movement," she claimed, "and the mind enriched by experience." Such statements imply that an aesthetic moment should comprise technique-instruction only. However, if, as she believed, "Nijinsky took thousands of leaps before the memorable one" (Gardner 1993, 298), it seems that an analysis of the circumstances that created the memorable one would help us more completely understand how the dance works.

Likewise, teaching artists' ability to investigate completely why they make the decisions they do, or how they reflect-in-action, might unravel the intricate and messy happenings that characterize applied theatre. Indeed, many of the great leaders in the field are able to reflect-in-action and articulate how they do so. There are any number of eminent practitioners who have achieved recognition because they can cogently and artistically identify what the decisive characteristics of sound work are and how these can be achieved. How, I wonder, can we achieve this cogency and artistry within evaluation reports? How can evaluations understand and articulate the purposes of applied theatre? Reflective practitioner inquiry, in my view, provides some assistance.

THE INTERVENTIONIST

Schön argues that the emphasis on the expert is a damaging one to the sustained competence of professionals. He highlights difficulties in mainstream research activity when university academics, for example, enter field settings as authoritative or expert figures. While those people might present exciting action research models, it is unclear how the reflective praxis of those in the field will benefit from them. In this book, Schön (1983) distinguishes his idea of the *reflective contract* from the dominant *traditional contract* when developing professional competence:

In the Traditional Contract	In the Reflective Contract
I put myself in the professional's hands and in doing this I gain a sense of security based on faith.	I join with the professional in making sense of my case, and in doing this I gain a sense of increased involvement and action.
I have the comfort of being in good hands. I need only comply with his [sic] advice and all will be well.	I can exercise some control over the situation. I am not wholly dependent on him [sic]; he [sic] is also dependent on information and action that only I can undertake.
I am pleased to be served by the best person available.	I am pleased to be able to test my judgments about his [sic] competence. I enjoy the excitement of discovery about his [sic] knowledge, about the phenomena of his [sic] practice, and about myself. (302)

In the applied theatre, we should not be inculcating an evaluation-research culture that conforms to the traditional contract. Applied theatre workers should be actively engaged in their own evaluations rather than dependent on some outside agency. For the most part, the outside agencies, or interventionists, are at a distinct disadvantage when examining applied theatre because they are not a part of the process of designing and implementing the project. In Schön's traditional contract, the applied theatre would be dependent on the interventionist to do the evaluations. However, in the reflective contract, the teaching artists, the participants, the wider applied theatre community would be directly engaged with the evaluation report.

Applied theatre must not fall victim to what much educational research became: visiting researchers who use the classroom as a laboratory to satisfy their own research interests. Eisner (1985) likens such approaches to "educational commando raids" wherein external evaluators enter classrooms for the briefest periods only to quickly "collect the data and to leave" (143). Outside experts often are employed by universities where job advancement depends on the research activity of its members, whereas the ongoing employment status of teachers in schools is tied to other criteria, notably teaching and service. The applied theatre teaching artists become more accomplished through their ability to investigate and to reflect on their landscape. Applied theatre must be quite wary of the experts who want to come in and instruct how programs must be designed.

The experts become the all-knowing interventionists capable of managing, directing, and evaluating action. Interventionists have been common in action research models and are co-opted by or who co-opt field-settings to conduct research (Orton 1994). For the most part, applied theatre teaching artists have not seen themselves as able to perform the intervention role themselves; they look to an outsider, a stranger to the field, to conduct the evaluation function. I am appealing for a participatory form of evaluation in which teaching artists engage in a process of self-inquiry with the participants.

While interventionists are incorporated within reflective practitioner design, Schön construes their role as a mentoring one in which the talents of all parties inform the research act. Power and control come from a sense of ownership and the belief that each player can provide important input to effective praxis. Applied theatre can benefit from outside agents who come in to guide and support a project, but the agents should work in partnership with teaching artists, acting as collaborators not autocrats. Even though I am not entirely convinced teaching artists are incapable of performing the role of interventionist—in other words, that they are incapable of pressing devices through which they individually can address their own questions into their work—I do believe Schön's reflective contract (teaching artists collaborate with outside interventionists) can be an invaluable educative experience.

AN INTERPRETIVE-BASED PARADIGM FOR EVALUATORS

When engaged in this kind of a reflective contract, where the individual voices and experiences of teaching artists and participants are central to competency and effectiveness, it is apparent that it is better to seek out the mechanisms for collecting and analyzing

data from within a narrative tradition. Just as Eisner feared the
Rambo-style educational commando raids, which university em-
ployees seemed to direct on schools, I fear the tightly "conducted"
experiments that endeavor to numerically render human experience. "Educational practice," concurs Eisner (1985), "is an inor-
dinately complicated affair filled with contingencies that are
extremely difficult to predict, let alone control" (104). Similarly,
the field settings where applied theatre takes place are complex
units that cannot be neatly controlled.

The unpredictable nature of applied theatre demands that preconceived notions of planning be constantly reevaluated in action. Unpredictability and uncertainty removes us from the world
of singular truth and plunges us into multiple realities and multiple visions. It is this multiplicity that is at the heart of reflective
practitioner design. How then is this multiplicity best evaluated?

It will come as no surprise that the kind of reflective praxis I am
advocating for in this book yields insights most effectively when
the techniques used in ethnography are used. Ethnography's history
is situated within cultural anthropology and is exemplified in the
work of field researchers such as Franz Boas, Bronislaw Malinowski,
Margaret Mead, and Clifford Geertz who would enter isolated communities and describe an aspect of cultural life. Their "thick," or
rich, descriptions are grounded in a natural setting where observed
events would not be distorted by clinical measurements often pursued in a positivist or neopositivist tradition. Because ethnogra-
phers maintain that a primary feature of human social life is that
its individuals are continually interpreting and making sense of
their world, any investigation of that world must relate these interpretations to the natural everyday situations in which people live
(Hitchcock & Hughes 1995, 28).

In the arts, there are numerous examples of works that are interested in the power of ethnography to provide comprehensive
insights into artistic processes. As we saw with Kaufman's "The
Laramie Project," there is increasing interest in what is referred to
as *performed ethnography*—taking the life stories of people and rendering them into dramatic presentations. To a certain extent, this
is what we are doing in the applied theatre, and this was the case
in the domestic violence project described in Chapter 4. We draw
on the experiences of a range of people as we recreate moments

from their lives for others to contemplate and interrogate (Goldstein 2003).

In Eve Ensler's (1999) "The Vagina Monologues," we have an example of a dramatic text that captures the experiences of women and their experiences of sex and sexuality. As the women in the Ensler work recall their lives while growing up, experimenting with sex, and enduring the various taboos associated with their genitalia, the playwright hopes old wounds will be healed and greater tolerance will be forthcoming:

> But "The Vagina Monologues" goes beyond purging a past full of negative attitudes. It offers a personal, grounded-in-the-body way of moving toward the future. I think readers, men as well as women, may emerge from these pages not only feeling more free within themselves—and about each other—but with alternatives to the old patriarchal dualism of feminine/masculine, body/mind, and sexual/spiritual that is rooted in the division of our physical selves into "the part we talk about" and the "the part we don't." (xvi)

This work has played to packed houses throughout the world, although it is not to everyone's taste given its graphic and sometime shocking descriptions of the abuses women have endured over time. I remember one year I proposed a scene from the text as an audition piece for incoming undergraduates who wanted to major in applied theatre; however, even in this setting, it was felt that the material was too controversial—the very mention of the word *vagina* was considered risqué! Nonetheless, the accounts the women provide in the play are reflective commentaries on their lives and the times, and through these stories, we are further drawn into the condition of what it means to live.

In evaluating the applied theatre, we should draw on narrative accounts of human affairs as a way of exposing and examining the truths people have constructed for themselves. Evaluations should be written in an accessible style, which opens up for the reader or the listener what occurred in the applied theatre. We must try and avoid the deathly treatise that does not help convey the spirit of the applied theatre. Accounts of applied theatre can be boring to read if effort is not taken to seek the most appropriate phrase, to select an eloquent metaphor, to write with an engaging narrative style to artfully capture the lived experiences.

In British theatre, for example, Anthony Sher's *Year of the King* (1985) is a fascinating account of how he grew into the role of Richard III when he was rehearsing Shakespeare's play for the Royal Shakespeare Company. Sher's account assumes a reflective practitioner's style as he projects himself into the role and shares with his readers the substance of his interventions during the rehearsal process. In the work of Constantin Stanislavski ([1949] 1987) at the Moscow Arts Theatre earlier this century, we can even see a passion in case study and how the intense description of a rehearsal process can demonstrate the skills of artists and artistry. In this kind of work, less is more seems to be a tenet, which probably accounts for the widespread use of case studies when presenting ethnographic accounts.

It would be difficult to write evaluations of applied theatre without including accounts of those who experience it; these accounts give body to the report. Like performed ethnography, the reflective practitioner recognizes that reality is multiple and shifting and that truths evolve and transform over time. Applied theatre evaluators are not so much interested in testing a preconceived hypothesis, but rather in allowing the data to generate a hypothesis. This latter distinction is a particularly important one. Questions, dilemmas, and uncertainties can evolve in process. As Georges Seurat in the Sondheim musical discovers the images for his canvas through the experience of creativity, evaluators of applied theatre must be open to transformed worlds.

Evaluators tend to be interested in broad questions such as the following:

- *How does applied theatre speak to this community?*
- *What do the participants in the applied theatre project understand the dilemmas, the issues, the topics to be?*
- *How successful was the applied theatre in investigating these topics?*
- *How do teaching artists engage participants with the work?*

The evaluation questions inevitably might change once observations commence, as indeed they should if the evaluator is to be open to the range of diverse interactions that inform an applied theatre event.

In my experience, the broader the question, the less likely the evaluator will be able to script a schedule of predetermined categories and codes through which data can be collected and analyzed. The danger in such a script is that it locks the evaluation into testing hypotheses or researching problems, and thereby prevents the possibility to be open to the multiplicity of happenings and events that can occur in the field site.

The action research models can pivot on quite a different proposition than the one I am proposing in this chapter; according to Orton (1994):

> Action Research begins with a problem in the practice of a person or group of persons. The problem normally appears as ineffectiveness: a practitioner does X with the intention of achieving Y. Y does not occur. *Non-Y* (what does occur) is unacceptable. The practitioner is thus faced with the dilemma of wanting to achieve Y but only knowing how to produce *non-Y*. (86)

While I do not want to undermine the importance of teaching artists investigating problems within their field settings, a difficulty in aligning these problems to ineffectiveness is that it can promote a simplistic cause–effect view of human experience. Testing hypotheses could prevent an openness to hypothesis generation. For example, let's take a classroom study which, while not an applied theatre project, highlights the concerns I am raising.

In a study, which aimed to test whether creative drama affected the quality of narrative writing in second and third graders in Utah, the investigators were constrained by their evaluation design. The experimental constraints produced a rigid inflexibility and, in certain instances, stifled participants' interest. The fact that the children were presented with a series of exercises, which had to be completed within specific time limits, with predetermined outcomes meant that evaluators' observations were locked into measuring one theory. "These observations," they mused regretfully, "suggest that drama might be a more successful planning activity under naturalist conditions" (Moore & Caldwell 1990, 18). Their dependence on testing a hypothesis within conventional understandings of empirical design distorted their ability to allow natural events to unfold around them.

Action research, committed to concrete solutions to immediate problems, could unintentionally promote a view that conflicts can be resolved, that truth can be found, and that life can be controlled.

Perhaps it is the word *problem* that worries me here; I suppose I am more interested in how evaluations can explore possibilities and raise an agenda rather than test a problem. In this respect, I agree with Maxine Greene (1989, 215): if artists are for disclosing the extraordinary in the ordinary, then evaluations should include the troubling questions artworks often raise. Just as Greene is interested in how artists transfigure the commonplace, I want to explore how reflective practitioners are reading their world; how they make decisions about importance and value; how they struggle with ambiguity and contradiction; and how they begin to ascertain the logical procedures through which they will collect, analyze, and present that struggle. I am interested, then, in the human dimension present in applied theatre evaluations and the questions this dimension implies for an evaluation design.

THE ART OF EVALUATION

In this chapter, I am arguing that the most effective evaluators are those who also operate as reflective practitioners. I am also encouraging teaching artists to be directly involved in the evaluation of applied theatre. A recurring myth is that studies that include narrative accounts of reflective practitioners lack the hard-edge of reports informed by numerical renderings of human experience. Numbers, it seems, are more credible than descriptions of people and their work. Reflective practitioner design challenges this myth in two primary ways: the reflective practitioner is the principal instrument for mediating data; and, multiple perspectives on the event researched, what is now referred to as *crystallization*, confirm the trustworthiness of the findings.

The Human Instrument

In one of the most engaging accounts on the art of acting, *Building a Character*, Stanislavaski ([1949] 1987) demonstrates his understanding of art not by discretely listing the features of acting technique but by presenting the diary of Kostya, a fictitious student. Kostya's diary, a comprehensive record and novelistic account of the experiences of a group of actors with their director, Tortsov, enables Stanislavki to probe the world of characterization through the hearts and minds of a troupe of dedicated performers.

At the beginning of our lesson I told Tortsov, the Director of our school and theatre, that I could comprehend with my mind the process of planting and training within myself the elements necessary to create character, but that it was still unclear to me how to achieve the building of that character in physical terms. Because, if you do not use your body, your voice, a manner of speaking, walking, moving, if you do not find a form of characterization which corresponds to the image, you probably cannot convey to others its inner, living system. (3)

The scope of Stanislavski's intent is beyond the focus of this chapter; however, a recurring theme of his work, which relates to reflective practitioner design, is the centrality of the human instrument in the collection, analysis, and presentation of data. Just as the actor explores the human condition and probes how the body can most powerfully represent that condition, reflective practitioners too draw on their own understanding of human affairs.

Reflective practitioners use their instrument, themselves, to raise questions of inquiry, to process how those questions will be investigated, and to consider how emergent findings will impact upon their lifelong work. Like qualitative research design, there is a recognition that "the field research process is as much concerned with the hopes, fears, frustrations and assumptions" of those participating in the evaluation act (Burgess 1985, 2).

Reflective practitioners fundamentally resist the idea of an externally driven agenda. Applied theatre evaluations should be generated from the field as a result of issues teaching artists, in part, formulate. In reflective practitioner design, our work, our life experiences, become the vehicle for exploration of a lived event.

Logbooks

If the human instrument is the principal medium for raising the agenda in reflective practitioner research, then the logbook is the place where that agenda is recorded. This habit is one informed from anthropology in which field notes and dedicated entries in logbooks become a pivotal feature in data collection and analysis. Diaries, journals, or portfolios have a long-established tradition in artistic praxis; throughout time, the artist's need to make sense of experience by recording a relationship to an event or process has been integral to cultural expression. Artist's records are not only written composites but can include a range of media.

I am reminded of the intricate designs Rudolf Laban (Haynes 1987) drew of his dances, which enabled him to construct a visual formulae of his technique. The haunting images of spidery webs and bottleneck toads drawn by Anthony Sher enabled him to un-derstand the workings of Richard III's mind and provided a gateway into characterization. Howard Gardner (1993) reminds us of how Martha Graham's creative life was powered by her conscientious and obsessive cataloguing, which would occupy evenings of intense activity. Graham is an especially good example of how logbooks can interact with reflective practice. "Her heroine St. Denis," writes Gardner, "had always scribbled down words, essays and poems, from which her dances had somehow emerged." Readers can only spec-ulate whether Graham's poetic imaginings would have danced on stage had she not embarked on the Denis-inspired comprehensive portfolio inquiry described in the following reflection:

> I get the ideas going. Then I write down, I copy out of any books that stimulate me at the time many quotations and I keep it. And I put down the source. Then when it comes to the actual work I keep a complete record of the steps. I keep notes of every dance I have. I don't have notations. I just put it down and know what the words mean, or what the movements mean and where you go and what you do and maybe an explanation here and there. (299)

In each case—Graham, Sher, and Laban—we see how the logbook becomes the tool for demonstrating the evolving understanding of particular phenomena. The logbook becomes a sourcebook, and recalls their evolving relationship to the work.

There are no shortcuts to keeping a logbook for this kind of evaluation. Because many leading qualitative researchers have written on this technique and its centrality to interpretive-based design, I will not repeat details of the works here (Ely 1991, Eisner 1991, Hitchcock & Hughes 1995, Lincoln & Guba 1985). In my experience, however, those evaluators who are unable to keep their logbooks in a timely and ongoing manner are disadvantaged when they analyze and/or write up their data. It is difficult to record your observations of an applied theatre event that occurred days, months, even years ago, let alone attempt to analyze those observations. The trick it seems is to follow Graham's lead and become passionate about the study and want to put it on the public record where it can be scrutinized and where it can direct, hopefully, further action.

Two further methods used in interpretive-based design are interviews and journals, and I now turn to these to illustrate how they can be employed in applied theatre evaluations.

Interviews and Journals

When seeking feedback on the applied theatre, evaluators can endeavor to interview or talk to participants to check on how they are responding to and interpreting the work. While it sometimes can be difficult to arrange permission to interview those who participate in the applied theatre, evaluation reports that do not include their experiences lack detail. Securing necessary authorizations from participants permits evaluators to use their words and descriptions in reports. Because reports sometimes are published and/or included in articles about the applied theatre, it is especially important for participants to know how what they say may be used in the professional arena.

Interviews are an especially rich form of data collection because they permit evaluators to follow-up hunches, to probe complexity, and to understand why certain behaviors were demonstrated. Sometimes it is not immediately clear why participants respond in the manner they do during the applied theatre; expressions of shock or surprise may be misread by teaching artists. Simply describing participants' behaviors is not enough, especially if those behaviors are seen as significant during the applied theatre.

In a sense, evaluations should try to get on the inside of participants' and teaching artists' heads. It is helpful to know what drove particular actions, gestures, stances. Interviews can assist in developing another perspective on the work. By soliciting different applied theatre observations—seeking another insight or slant on the event—we come closer to, and develop confidence in, the authenticity of the findings and recommendations evaluation reports can yield.

In some instances, interviews can be quite revealing, particularly if the interviewer can gain the trust of the interviewee, and then ask open-ended questions like the following:

- *What did you find interesting about the applied theatre?*
- *What were you puzzled by?*
- *Were you surprised by anything?*
- *What didn't work?*
- *Which strategies did you think were most effective? Least effective?*
- *If this program was to be revised, what suggestions would you have?*
- *If you were to evaluate this program, what criteria would you use?*

It would be fair to say that there has been very little written on participants' responses to the applied theatre. In the past, such documentation has been rare and most of the emphases of writing about applied theatre have been through the teaching artists' eyes. Readers have had to put their faith in the author of these studies and assume that the observations are credible. However, if these observations are the only ones informing the development and direction of the applied theatre, it is possible that conclusions may be skewed or too overtly value-laden. Readers of evaluation reports need to believe that the evidence on which conclusions are drawn is convincing.

Interviewing participants and others associated with the applied theatre acts as a distancing strategy—evaluators can be removed from the data and look at it with new eyes. Just as Brecht fears the overwhelming appeal to emotion prevalent in conventional theatre forms, evaluations should not be drawn from one perspective only. Interviewing is a time-consuming process and one that I am unable to do justice to here. I would argue though that applied theatre evaluators need to develop very effective interviewing skills and consider the variety of questioning techniques that have informed interpretive-based design (Lofland & Lofland 1984; Minichiello, Aroni, Timewell, & Alexander 1991).

Interviews do not need to be conducted just one-on-one. Focus group interviews, which can be audio- or videotaped, can help generate the major themes participants experienced as they engaged in the piece. Remember though, you need permission from the group before you can collect such data. A focus group tends to brainstorm issues around what the applied theatre participants and others experienced; this brainstorming can serve as a basis for more critical inquiry. The following are examples of questions to use:

What struck you about the hotseating strategy?
To what extent did you find the teaching artist believable as that character?
What surprised you about the forum theatre technique?
What discoveries did you make through the forum theatre?
What would you change in the program?
How might this program be of benefit to the community?

One strength of the focus group is that you are gaining multiple perspectives on the applied theatre. Sometimes it can be easier for participants to open up when they are with others. In communities where there are strong storytelling traditions, the focus group builds on those traditions and honors the narrative modes so prevalent in that society. "Rich" talk can help sharpen ideas and multiple inputs can tighten perspectives.

It is sometimes useful to ask participants to jot down notes and record their observations of the images, the moments, the actions, the discoveries that influenced them while they were observing the applied theatre. This is not always possible, especially in communities where there might be strong resistance to the written word. Nonetheless, it might be possible to target interested individuals to help you learn more about how effective the applied theatre was. When participants realize the information they provide is actually beneficial to you and to the future of the applied theatre, usually they will eagerly cooperate and keep a journal. I know that when I work in classroom settings, for instance, and embark on evaluation projects detailing how theatre can enliven school curriculum, and when students are asked to be coevaluators and know their viewpoints are necessary and vital, they are more likely to assist in the formal collection of data. Again though, remember that when using this data in evaluation reports, written permission of the participant must be sought.

Journals written by participants can provide more reflective opportunities for ideas to be developed. A written journal demands a contemplative encounter in which participants, with their notebooks in hand, formulate reactions to particular aspects of the work. The evaluators might give questions for the participants to address or the participants might be asked to reflect on their own questions or to write entries that are more or less stream of consciousness. I know that journals can be used in haphazard ways, and that sometimes they yield very little informative data; the trick is to find participants whom you believe would enjoy helping in this way.

Although some might question the ethics of paying participants to keep a journal, I know of a few instances in which teaching artists have budgeted money to reimburse participants for the time it takes to keep journals. Financial reimbursement, however, could very well impact on the content of the journal because participants might feel a need to be supportive of the program if they are receiving a fee for keeping the journal. This is exactly the same dilemma external evaluators face when commissioned by an agency that has an investment in the future success of the applied theatre. How can external evaluators be neutral when they are being paid to evaluate?

Journals can become powerful devices for providing another perspective on the work; like the interview, they can invite participants to expose their evolving relationship. In a project with Chinese American children, for example, I encouraged them to keep journals after I shared my logbook with them. I told them that because my log consisted of my perceptions of what occurred in the field, it would be helpful if I could read their written perceptions too. My observations, I admitted, would probably be quite different from theirs. Any subject of interest, or uninterest for that matter, could be written on a voluntary basis—the children were not to feel co-opted into writing the journal, which would not be graded (Taylor 1998).

Interviewing participants and finding insightful ways of using their journals demonstrate the detailed attempts pursued by evaluators as they search for understanding. Observations in logbooks are part of this search, and often the interview data and other artifacts collected are entered there so that the evaluator has a complete record. The more avenues of inquiry the evaluation report can tap into, the more perspectives sought, the more likely the conclusions will be well-informed and authentic.

I've only focused on two data-collection methods here, ignoring the application of audiovisual resources and the widespread use of computer technology that can be employed when evaluating the applied theatre (Tesch 1990). Readers need to research the variety of techniques and strategies open to them and be prepared to discover their own. These discoveries, though, must still be cognizant of participants' rights and the need to have their identity protected. The days of entering field settings and describing community happenings without written permission are long gone. Such agreement usually entails consent from all relevant parties, including primary caregivers in the case of minors, as to how the observations are going to be analyzed and presented. Applied theatre participants should have the right to say no to a proposed inquiry and to be provided with opportunities to respond positively or negatively to any description of the work before it enters the public arena.

But, we should not let these necessary clearances and matters of ethics stifle our reflective journey; indeed, they should liberate reflective practitioners into engaging the wider community in their investigations. The more people who take ownership, the more change is possible. It seems clear that there is complete freedom when our motives are shared, our hopes are revealed, and our frustrations are explored.

THE ART OF CRYSTALLIZATION

When attempting to determine whether the evaluation report is a credible document, teaching artists should endeavor to confirm that their observations and recordings are indeed authentic. An observation does not necessarily have credibility because many people confirm it. The trick is to ensure that the data collected has an internal logic and reads as a credible account of what occurred in the field. Just because one person says the applied theatre was "great" does not necessarily mean this holds true for the entire group of participants. Besides, one needs to probe further what is meant by "great." *Great* can mean different things to different people: Were the concepts interrogated important? Did the participant change any preconceived ideas that she or he might have had about those concepts? Was the staging "great"? The singing? Evaluators need to get behind what is motivating the participants to respond in the manner they do.

Sometimes the lone voice who disagrees with the crowd has made just as perceptive an observation as the others. Individuals' voices need to be included in reports about the applied theatre because they provide balance and credibility to the observations.

Some evaluators discuss the important need to triangulate findings, to confirm the accuracy or credibility of a particular viewpoint by seeking corroboration. We must find different ways of achieving truthfulness other than a method that basically says, "Well, it must be correct for three people said it!" Laurel Richardson (2000) has been particularly helpful on this point:

> In triangulation, a researcher deploys "different methods"—such as interviews, census data, and documents—to "validate" findings. These methods however carry the same domain assumptions, including the assumption that there is a "fixed point" or "object" that can be triangulated. But in postmodernist mixed-genre texts, we do not triangulate; we crystallize. We recognize that there are far more than "three sides" from which to approach the world. (934)

"Crystal" serves as a good metaphor, for while it contains "symmetry and substance" (934), it contains a variety of different shapes and patterns and both refracts and reflects. "What we see depends upon our angle of repose," argues Richardson. Our view of the world is manipulated by the perspective from where we sit, by the lens through which we see. "Ingeniously," about crystals she adds that as we hold them and observe them, "we know there is always more to know" (934). Each angle of repose opens up a new vista, an alternate way of reading the world. What is especially eloquent about the notion of crystallization is that it opens us up to new possibilities of seeing, and new ways of knowing.

We are always on a journey of discovery. This journey is certainly what is powering applied theatre. We can never be certain that our hunches about human behavior are correct. Participants can respond differently at different presentations; what seemed apparent at one moment was not apparent in another. As we attempt to crystallize the various perspectives around applied theatre, evaluations should take the multiple and shifting perspectives of teaching artists, participants, and the wider community that has a vested interest in the program into account. Evaluations should include interview data, journal writing, descriptions of behavior, anecdotes from participants, funders' expectations and hopes. The evaluation report should be a multitext narrative, which privileges all voices and is especially eager to solicit the voices of the silent.

The best evaluators act as participants–observers who can speak from a variety of perspectives, and they need to be experienced and detached. Distance is necessary, of course, because it enables evaluators to step back and look closely; distance enables a possible new perspective on a familiar event, a rethinking of an ingrained belief. Crystallization makes the familiar strange; it decenters the evaluator from the lived event and provides a valuable opportunity to hear other voices and see new faces while building a comprehensive understanding of a complex event.

Defamiliarization is not a foreign concept to the applied theatre. To make the familiar strange is what an applied theatre event is about so that participants can explore recognizable occurrences through new eyes. Crystallization operates on the same principle. Teaching artists are forever seeking a new twist on a familiar event, a different way to manipulate the form to express or demonstrate an idea.

In the theatre, many playwrights and directors, such as Antonin Artaud, Harold Pinter, and Samuel Beckett, have worked against convention, exploring unique relationships between form and content. We could liken their works to reflective praxis in which artists set the agenda, and then inquire deeply into an aspect of their craft. Just as artists look for theatrical techniques, which will alienate an audience from the artistic work so that they can understand it better, crystallization in interpretive design alienates evaluators from the data as they search for authenticity.

The great theatre genius, Bertolt Brecht, achieved archetypal status as someone interested in these notions of defamiliarization and crystallization as he sought distancing devices that would assist both actors and spectators understand the perspectives contained within his drama. Much has been written about Brecht's idea of an Epic Theatre and his various attempts to discover ways to detach the audience from the performance through the dramatic art form. Brecht was critical of orthodox theatre, which presented simplistic and saccharine solutions to life's problems and required a hallucinated participation of the spectators. His early work saw a growing commitment to exposing the machinery of the theatre to an audience so that they would not submit or lose themselves within the piece (Willet 1977):

> Give us some light on the stage, electrician. How can we
> Playwrights and actors put forward
> Our view of the world in half-darkness. The dim twilight
> Induces sleep. But we need the spectator's
> Wakeful, even watchfulness. . . . (161)

Applied theatre is filled with workers who share Brecht's concern and dream for devices that can activate participants' contemplative powers. Like Brecht, Beckett was a master at presenting bleak, desolate, often humorous depictions of the world that would challenge the viewer to work hard to have a relationship with the text. They both share applied theatre artists' desire to shake the audience out of possible dreamy states and to become more alert to how the world is operating and how they operate in it. These alert states, what Greene (1989) refers to as participants' wide-awakeness, should be shared by those who come to evaluate the applied theatre.

Applied theatre evaluation is a most important process, but it must be done with integrity and for the right reasons. There should be no clumsy data collection and analysis in any evaluation. Evaluations should occur while a program is in process, and they require a concentrated effort to acquire data as the applied theatre project evolves.

Evaluation during an applied theatre can put us back in touch with our streams of consciousness. Through evaluation, we can listen to our needs and to those of participants, perhaps seeing the work from the perspective of someone else for the first time, or understanding how a strategy really did or did not work with a particular population. Evaluators, like good reflective practitioners, can remove the stifling shackles of expertise when writing reports and revise conventional understandings of authority. They can interrogate the truths they confront daily and imagine what is possible in the field, what is not possible, and what might be. I cannot think of a more valuable investigative approach when evaluating applied theatre than the challenges presented by becoming a reflective practitioner.

WORKS CITED

Ackroyd, J. 2000. "Applied Theatre: Problems and Possibilities." *Applied Theatre Researcher*, 1, 1–12 (an electronic journal of the Centre for the Applied Theatre Research, Brisbane—available at www.gu.edu.au/centre/atr).

Ahmed, S. J. 2002. "Wishing for a World Without 'Theatre for Development': Demystifying the Case for Bangladesh." *Research in Drama Education (RIDE)* 7 (2), 207–19.

Albee. E. 1965. *Who's Afraid of Virginia Woolf?* Harmondsworth: Penguin.

Albert, J. 2001, March 10–11. "Body of Evidence." *The Weekend Australian* (newspaper), pp. R18–R19.

Argyris, C., and D. Schön. 1974. *Theory in Practice: Increasing Professional Effectiveness.* San Francisco: Jossey-Bass.

Ball, S. 1999. "Playing on the Margins: Creating Safe Spaces Through the Arts." *NADIE Journal* 23 (2), 27–32.

Beckerman, B. 1970. *Dynamics of Drama.* New York: Knopf.

Best, D., M. Greene, and M. Grumet. 1998. Presentation at School Reform Through the Arts, international seminar, New York University. In *Applied Theatre Researcher* (an electronic journal of the Centre for Applied Theatre Research, Brisbane—available at www.gu.edu.au /centre/atr).

Boal, A. 1985. *Theatre of the Oppressed.* New York: Theatre Communications Group.

———. 1995. *The Rainbow of Desire. The Boal Method of Theatre and Therapy.* London: Routledge.

———. 2001. *Hamlet and the Baker's Son: My Life in Theatre and Politics.* London: Routledge.

Bolton, G. 1979. *Towards a Theory of Drama in Education.* Essex: Longman.

———. 1985. "Changes in Thinking About Drama in Education." *Theory into Practice* XXIV (3), 151–57.

———. 2003. *Dorothy Heathcote's Story: The Biography of a Remarkable Drama Teacher.* Stoke-on-Trent: Trentham Books.

Burgess, R. 1985. *Field Methods in the Study of Education.* London: Falmer.

Byam, D. L. 1999. *Community in Motion: Theatre for Development in Africa.* London: Bergin and Garvey.

Cohen-Cruz, J. 1998. *Radical Street Performance: An International Anthology.* London: Routledge.

Day, B. 1996. *This Wooden "O": Shakespeare's Globe Reborn*. London: Oberon Books.

Dobson, W., T. Goode, and A. Boyd. 2000. "Knowing Who We Are (and That We Are Not Alone)." In *Drama for Life*, edited by J. O'Toole and M. Lepp, 189–98. Brisbane: Playlab Press.

Doyle, C. 1993. *Raising Curtains on Education: Drama as a Site for Critical Pedagogy*. Westport, CT: Bergin and Garvey.

Eisner, E. 1985. *The Art of Educational Evaluation*. Philadelphia: Falmer.

———. 1991. *The Enlightened Eye: Qualitative Inquiry and the Enchantment of Educational Practice*. New York: Macmillan.

Ely, M., M. Anzul, T. Friedman, D. Garner, and A. M. Steinmetz. 1991. *Doing Qualitative Research: Circles Within Circles*. London: Falmer.

Ensler, E. 1999. *The Vagina Monologues*. New York: Villard.

Freire, P. 1970. *Pedagogy of the Oppressed*. New York: Continuum.

Garcia, L. 2001. " 'Finding One's Own Way' Through a Radical Critical Pedagogy." *Applied Theatre Researcher* (2), 1–10 (an electronic journal of the Centre for Applied Theatre Research, Brisbane—available at www.gu.edu.au/centre/atr).

Gardner, H. 1993. *Creating Minds: An Anatomy of Creativity Seen Through the Lives of Freud, Einstein, Picasso, Stravinsky, Eliot, Graham, and Gandhi*. New York: Basic Books.

Goldstein, T. 2003. *Teaching and Learning in a Multilingual School Community: Choices, Risks and Dilemmas*. Mahwah, NJ: Lawrence Erlbaum Associates.

Grady, S. 2000. *Drama and Diversity: A Pluralistic Perspective for Educational Drama*. Portsmouth, NH: Heinemann.

Greene, M. 1978. *Landscapes of Learning*. New York: Teachers College Press.

———. 1989. "Art Worlds in Schools." In *The Symbolic Order*, edited by P. Abbs, 213–24. London: Falmer,

———. 1999. "Releasing the Imagination." *NJ (National Journal of Drama, Australia)* 23, 9–18.

Greenwood, J. 2001. "Within a Third Space." *RIDE* 6 (1), 193.

Harris, T. 2001, April 9. "Young Often See Mothers Bashed." *The Australian*, p. 3.

Haynes, A. 1987. "The Dynamic Image: Changing Perspectives in Dance Education." In *Living Powers: The Arts in Education*, edited by P. Abbs, 141–62. London: Falmer.

Hitchcock, G., and D. Hughes. 1995. *Research and the Teacher*, Second Edition. London: Routledge.

Jackson, A. 1993. *Learning Through Theatre: New Perspectives on Theatre in Education*. London: Routledge.

———. 2000. "Inter-acting with the Past—The Use of Participatory Theatre at Museum and Heritage Sites." *RIDE* 5 (2), 199–216.

Kaufman, M. 2001. *The Laramie Project*. New York: Dramatists Play Service Inc.

Landy, R. 1986. *Drama Therapy: Concepts and Practices*. Springfield: Charles C. Thomas.

———. 1993. *Persona and Performance: The Meaning of Role in Drama, Therapy and Everyday Life*. Bristol, PA: Jessica Kingsley.

Lincoln, Y. S., and E. G. Guba. 1985. *Naturalistic Inquiry*. Newbury Park, CA: Sage.

Lofland, J., and L. Lofland. 1984. *Analyzing Social Settings: A Guide to Qualitative Observation and Analysis*. Belmont, CA: Wadsworth.

Martin, N. 1987. "On the Move." In *Reclaiming the Classroom*, edited by S. Goswami and P. Stillman, 20–27. Portsmouth, NH: Heinemann.

McKenna, T. 2001. "A Scenario." *Applied Theatre Researcher*, 2, 1–6 (an electronic journal of the Centre for Applied Theatre Research, Brisbane—available www.gu.edu.au/centre/atr).

McPherson, C. 1999. *The Weir and Other Plays*. New York: Theatre Communications Group.

Mda, Z. 1983. "When People Play People" (in Pompeo Nogueira, M. 2002. "Theatre for Development: An Overview"). *RIDE* 7 (1), 104–108.

Merkin, D. 1999. October 4. "Scoundrel Time." *The New Yorker*, pp. 110–11.

Minichiello, V., R. Aroni, E., Timewell, and L. Alexander. 1991. *In-Depth Interviewing*. Melbourne: Longman.

Moore, B. H., and H. Caldwell. 1990. "The Art of Planning" *Youth Theatre Journal*. 4 (3), 12–20.

Neelands, J., and T. Goode. 2000. *Structuring Drama Work: A Handbook of Available Forms in Theatre and Drama*. Cambridge: Cambridge University Press.

New South Wales (Australia). 2000. *Department of Housing Community Renewal Strategy Newsletter* 1 (1), Brochure (Lismore).

Nolte, J. 2000. "Re-experiencing Life." In *Drama for Life*, edited by J. O'Toole and M. Lepp, 209–21. Brisbane: Playlab Press.

O'Connor, P. 2001. "The Inaugural Research Institute of the Centre for Applied Theatre Research: A Personal Perspective." *Applied Theatre*

Researcher 2, 1–3 (an electronic journal of the Centre for Applied Theatre Research, Brisbane—available www.gu.edu.au/centre/atr).

Odhiambo, C. 2001. "The Gods Are Not to Blame: Theatre for Development and Societal Transformation." *NJ* 25 (2), 35–42.

Ogolla Nyangore, V. 2000. "Listen to Your Mothers: Theatre and Health in Village Settings." In *Drama for Life*, edited by J. O'Toole and M. Lepp, 77–84. Brisbane: Playlab Press.

O'Neill. C. 1995. *Drama Worlds: A Framework for Process Drama*. Portsmouth, NH: Heinemann.

Orton, J. 1994. "Action Research and Reflective Practice: An Approach to Research for Drama Educators." *International Research Issue, NADIE Journal* 18 (2), 85–96 (a publication of the National Association for Drama in Education, Australia).

O'Sullivan, C. 2001. "Searching for the Marxist in Boal." *RIDE* 6 (1), 85–97.

O'Toole, J., and B. Burton. 2002. "Cycles of Harmony: Action Research into the Effects of Drama on Conflict Management in Schools." *Applied Theatre Researcher* 3, 1–6 (an electronic journal of the Centre for Applied Theatre Research, Brisbane—available www.gu.edu.au /centre/atr).

Poe, E. A. 1979. *Forty-Two Tales*. London: Octopus Books.

Pompeo-Nogueira, M. 2002. "Theatre for Development: An Overview." *RIDE* 7 (1), 103–108, 202.

Rasmussen, B. 2000. "Applied Theatre and the Power Play—An International Viewpoint." *Applied Theatre Researcher*, 1, 1–4 (an electronic journal of the Centre for Applied Theatre Research, Brisbane—available www.gu.edu.au/centre/atr).

Richardson, L. 2000. "Writing: A Method of Inquiry." In *Handbook of Qualitative Research, Second Edition*, edited by N. Denzin and Y. Lincoln, 923–48. Thousand Oaks, CA: Sage.

Rodd, M. 1998. *Theatre for Community, Conflict and Dialogue: The Hope Is Vital Training Manual*. Portsmouth, NH: Heinemann.

Schön, D. 1983. *The Reflective Practitioner: How Professionals Think in Action*. New York: Basic Books.

Schonmann, S. 1996. "Jewish–Arab Encounters in the Drama/Theatre Class Battlefield." *RIDE* 1 (2), 175–88.

Shakespeare, W. 1957. *Hamlet*. New York: Washington Square Press.

———. 1963. *Macbeth*. New York: The New American Library.

Sher, A. 1985. *Year of the King*. London: Methuen.

Shewey, D. 2002, December 1. "A Play Has a Second Life as a Stage for Discussion." *The New York Times*, Section 2.

Smigiel, H. 1996. "Coming to Know: Naturalistic Inquiry in the Workplace." *RIDE* 1 (1), 95–103.

Sondheim, S., and B. Lapine. [1984] 1991. *Sunday in the Park with George.* New York: Applause.

Stanislavski, C. [1949] 1987. *Building a Character.* New York: Methuen.

Stenhouse, L. 1975. *Introduction to Curriculum Research and Development.* London: Heinemann.

Taylor, P. 1998. *Redcoats and Patriots: Reflective Practice in Drama and Social Studies.* Portsmouth, NH: Heinemann.

———. 2000. *The Drama Classroom: Action, Reflection, Transformation.* London: Routledge Falmer.

———. 2002a. "Afterthought: Evaluating Applied Theatre." *Applied Theatre Researcher* 3, 12–15 (an electronic journal of the Centre for Applied Theatre Research, Brisbane—available www.gu.edu.au /centre/atr).

———. 2002b. "The Applied Theatre: Building Stronger Communities." *Youth Theatre Journal* 16, 88–95.

———. 2003. "Musings on Applied Theatre: Toward a New Theatron." *Drama Magazine* 10 (2) May, 37–42.

Tesch, R. 1990. *Qualitative Research: Analysis Types and Software Tools.* London: Falmer.

Thompson, J. 2000. "Making a Break for It: Discourse and Theatre in Prisons." *Applied Theatre Researcher* 1, 1–5 (an electronic journal of the Centre for Applied Theatre Research, Brisbane—available www.gu.edu.au/centre/atr).

———. 2002. "Ugly, Unglamorous and Dirty: Theatre of Relief/ Reconciliation/Liberation in Places of War." *RIDE* 7 (1), 108–14.

Van Erven, E. 2001. *Community Theatre: Global Perspectives.* London: Routledge.

Vogel, P. 1998. *The Mammary Plays.* New York: Theatre Communications Group.

Winston, J. 2001. "Drug Education Through Creating Theatre in Education." *RIDE* 6 (1), 39–54.

Willet, J. 1977. *The Theatre of Bertolt Brecht: A Study from Eight Aspects.* London: Methuen.